———— Walks A
WORCEST

Broadway Tower, *the Worcestershire Plain behind,* (***Walk 13***).

Peter Kerr

First Published 1998

© Peter Kerr 1998

The walk descriptions, written to comply with the "Guidelines for Writers of Path Guides", issued by the Outdoor Writers' Guild, and the maps, were prepared on the dates listed. However, whilst every effort has been made to ensure accuracy, the author and publisher cannot accept any responsibility for any problems, or for any loss or injury, etc. resulting from the use of this book as, with time, changes to paths, stiles, etc. can occur, sometimes within months of the walk being researched.

The right of Peter Kerr to be identified as the author of this work has been asserted by him in accordance with the Copyright, Designs and Patent Act 1988.

The author records his thanks to the advertisers whose support has made the publication of this book possible. To Worcestershire County Council, both the Countryside and Conservation Services Section, for their considerable help in identifying suitable starting points and suggesting possible routes, and the Rights of Way Section, for help in making the Definitive Statements available and rectifying problems. Also to Olive, my wife, for typing and proof-reading, (blame her for any mistakes), and to Maria, Walter, and the County Council Rangers, who bravely went forth to try out the walks, and returned, so the descriptions must be correct!.

Books in print, by the same author:-

Walks Around Bewdley and the Wyre Forest - 1996
Walks Around The Severn Valley - 1997

Published by:-

Olpe Walking and Leisure Books
Dowles Road,
Bewdley,
Worcs. DY12 2EJ
Tel: 01299 403031

Artwork and Print by:-

Stargold Limited
Unit 2a, Mill Street,
Kidderminster,
Worcs. DY11 6XG
Tel: 01562 741603

ISBN 0-9525391-5-2

Walks Around **Worcestershire**

The **River Severn** *and* **Worcester Cathedral,** *(Walk 1).*

Walks Around **Worcestershire**

WALKS LOCATION MAP

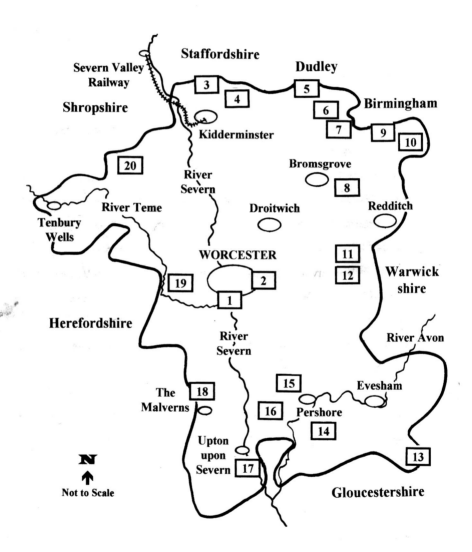

CONTENTS

INTRODUCTION and NOTES

Introduction

The reorganisation of Local Government in 1974 saw the merging of the then separate counties of Herefordshire and Worcestershire into one authority. Now, in April 1998, both counties re-emerge as separate entities. This book offers a variety of walks within the re-born county of Worcestershire, starting at the centre, the City of Worcester, and then to places on, or near to, the county boundary. The walks therefore show the variety of scenery that the county has for the walker to enjoy.

The County of Worcestershire, an area of 670 square miles, has a boundary with Shropshire, Staffordshire, Dudley, Birmingham, Warwickshire, Gloucestershire and, of course, Herefordshire. Three sizeable rivers run through the county, the Severn, which at 220 miles is the longest river in Britain, is joined by the Avon and the Teme, each with their own character and attractiveness. Also, around the boundary, are the raised areas of land offering viewpoints, such as the Clent, Waseley and Lickey Hills, Broadway Hill, Bredon Hill, Malvern Hills and the Abberley Hills. Thus the overall combination offers the rambler a variety of walking experiences.

With enjoyment and relaxation in mind most walks are relatively short, with some offering longer routes or a link with an adjacent walk, so most people, even the more energetic, should find suitable routes. Also, whilst the route notes have been written to give less experienced walkers the confidence to go into the countryside and find the correct 'Right of Way', (hence the detail), knowledgeable ramblers should find the route suggestions of interest.

All the walks and maps have been dated to show when they were researched and the notes prepared. At that date they were open and passable but, with time, changes occur. If problems are encountered, e.g. obstructed stiles, difficult crops, etc. these should be reported to the Worcestershire County Council, (see address on Page 9).

Walking and Recreational Facilities

The County Council have, over many years, developed a wide range of Country Parks, Picnic Places, etc., currently 25 in number, as well as long distance paths, (e.g. the Worcestershire Way). In addition there are also some shorter, informative, paths, (e.g. the Illey Way and the Icknield Way). Throughout the county, there are some 6240 Rights of Way covering 2900 miles, truly a paradise for ramblers, once they have been found. This book, with the help of the Countryside and Conservation Service Section of the County Council, uses a number of the above sites, and all the long distance routes are encountered. For reference these are listed on Page 7.

The Severn Way: A new long distance path following the River Severn from source to sea, (**Severn Trow** symbol). Encountered on **Walks 1 & 17**.

The Cotswold Way: A 100 mile National Trail, (Chipping Campden to Bath), passing through the county at Broadway. Encountered on **Walk 13**.

The Monarch's Way: A 610 mile path following the escape route, from Worcester to Shoreham, of Charles II in 1651. Encountered on **Walks 6, 7, 8 & 11**.

The Worcestershire Way: A 47 mile County Council regional route, (Kinver Edge to the Malvern Hills, **Pear** symbol). Encountered on **Walks 3, 18 & 19**.

North Worcestershire Path: A 26 mile County Council regional route following the northern boundary of the county, linking Kinver Edge with Majors Green near Solihull, (**Pine Cone** symbol). Encountered on **Walks 3, 4, 5, 7, 9 & 10**.

The Wychavon Way: A Wychavon District Council route of 42 miles from Holt Fleet to Winchcombe, (the '**W**' symbol). Encountered on **Walk 14**.

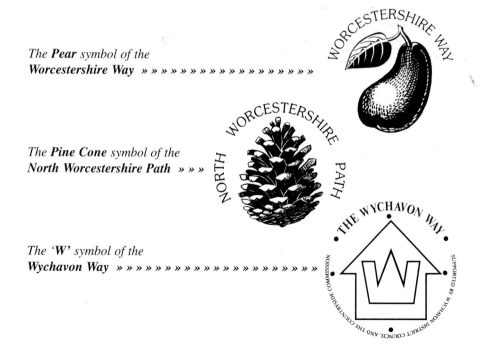

*The **Pear** symbol of the*
Worcestershire Way » » » » » » » » » » » » » » » » » »

*The **Pine Cone** symbol of the*
North Worcestershire Path » » »

*The '**W**' symbol of the*
Wychavon Way »

Refreshments

Places in Worcester City and other towns, etc. are not mentioned as they are too numerous. However, possible refreshment places on the routes have been listed.

General Notes

Times for walks are not given as each person/group walk at differing speeds. If in doubt use 2 miles/hour as a guide adding on stopping times, e.g. lunch. Also, please wear appropriate clothing/footwear and, to ensure co-operation from landowners, keep to public or permissive paths. Please follow the Country Code (see Page 9).

Route Maps and Ordnance Survey Maps

The **Route Maps**, based on information provided by the County Council, Birmingham City Council, The Woodland Trust, etc. and observations when researching the walks, are diagrammatic only, being intended as a general guide. They only show relevant features, e.g. fences, footbridges, pubs, etc., but not the overall area. The use of Ordnance Survey maps is strongly recommended and both the **Landranger**, (1.25 inch to 1 mile), and **Pathfinder**, (2.5 inch to 1 mile), maps are listed for each Route. The Pathfinder maps, which will be replaced by the **Explorer** range over the coming years, are far superior for walking purposes.

The start, (or finish), of the **Worcs. Way** *and the* **North Worcs. Path**, *(Walk 3).*

8

Country Code

Enjoy the countryside and respect its life and work.

Keep to public footpaths: Guard against all risk of fire:
Keep dogs under close control: Fasten all gates:
Leave livestock, crops and machinery alone: Take your litter home:
Protect wildlife, plants and trees: Help keep all water clean:
Take special care on country roads: Make no unnecessary noise:
Use gates and stiles to cross fences, hedges and walls:

Notes on Legal Aspects

There is considerable legislation regarding Rights of Way and the following are only very brief guidelines.

Any member of the public has a legal right of passage over a Public Right of Way. They may stop and admire the scenic views but not unduly linger or interfere with the rights, occupation or privacy of the landowner. A **footpath** (yellow waymark) is for use by people on foot only. A **bridleway** (blue waymark) is for use by people on foot or horseback and also on pedal cycles (but **not** motor cycles or mopeds).

Landowners have a legal obligation to facilitate the right of passage on Public Rights of Way across their land. Providing both parties respect each others rights ramblers should be able to enjoy the countryside with minimum disruption to landowners.

County Councils have a record of all the Rights of Way in the county on a list of **Definitive Maps**, and they are responsible for ensuring that the paths are open for public use. Any problems, etc. encountered on paths included in this book should be reported to Worcestershire County Council as listed below.

Worcestershire County Council
Rights of Way Section
County Hall
Spetchley Road
Worcester
Worcestershire
WR5 2NP

Tel. 01905 763763

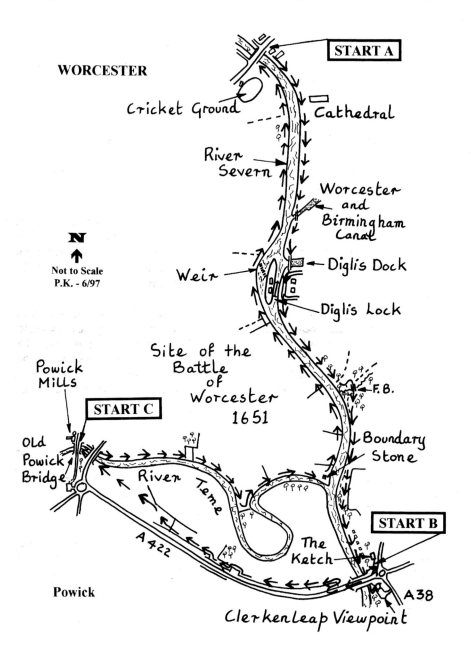

WORCESTER

Cricket Ground

Cathedral

River Severn

Worcester and Birmingham Canal

START A

Diglis Dock

Weir

Diglis Lock

N

Not to Scale
P.K. - 6/97

Site of the Battle of Worcester 1651

Powick Mills

START C

F.B.

Boundary Stone

Old Powick Bridge

River Teme

START B

A 422

The Ketch

Powick

A 38

Clerkenleap Viewpoint

WALK 1 WORCESTER and POWICK BRIDGE via the   6.5 Miles
RIVER SEVERN and the RIVER TEME

Start: A choice of three starting points, Worcester Bridge, **START A**, (GR. 846548); by The Ketch inn, **START B**, (GR. 853517); or the Old Powick Bridge, **START C**, (GR. 835525).

Parking: See details in **General Notes**, below.

Refreshments: Many places in Worcester and The Ketch at **START B**.

O.S. Maps: Pathfinder map 996 (Worcester) and Landranger map 150 (Worcester & The Malverns).

Summary: A walk with many historical connections, following the River Severn past Worcester Cathedral, the Worcester & Birmingham Canal and Diglis Lock. The route also includes old Powick Bridge, the River Teme and the site of the Battle of Worcester, (1651). A quick revision of local history, and a visit to The Commandery, would make this walk more enjoyable. Number of stiles:- 13.

General Notes: Space does not permit detailed history notes as well as detailed Route Notes, so on this walk a local history book would make a good companion. The walk lists three possible starting points. By **START A** there is chargeable parking; by **START B** there is free parking at the Clerkenleap Viewpoint. At the Old Powick Bridge, **START C**, there was, at the time of research, no official parking, this may change in the future so it is included as a start point for the walk.

Route Notes:

From Worcester Bridge, START A: From the City Centre side of the bridge follow the River Severn downstream, this first section, to **START B**, is along the **Severn Way**, (**SW**), with the Severn Trow symbols. See notes on Page 7. Initially the route passes boat moorings, (river trips), Worcester Cathedral, (pleasant gardens, note also the flood markings by the steps), and the Diglis Hotel.

Continue on the **SW** crossing over the entrance to the Worcester and Birmingham Canal. (The canal was built in the 1790s, is 30 miles long, has 58 locks, including the famous Tardebigge flight of 30 locks in 2.5 miles, and also five tunnels). (See also **Walk 8**). Keep following the River Severn past a factory complex (long drop to the river), pass over Diglis Dock and at the road turn right. Pass Diglis Lock and then leave the road to continue on the riverside path, now in more open countryside.

About 800 yards past the lock the path goes left, for some 100 yards, to follow a small stream before crossing it by a footbridge. Once over turn right and follow the path back to the River Severn, (the wider path is the **SW**). Continue on the riverside path, enter a caravan park and then pass boat moorings, (the Right of Way is close to the river and not through the caravans). Join a gravel path to pass under the road bridge. (At one time there was a ferry here, just below the site of The Ketch inn).

Go past the bridge for 40 yards, turn sharp left, leaving the **SW**, and go uphill and under the road bridge again. Cross a stile to the roadside, The Ketch is just to the left, and the Clerkenleap Viewpoint is across the dual carriageway over to the right.

From "The Ketch" inn, START B: From the roundabout cross the bridge on the upstream, (right), side and once across go sharp right and down a concrete ramp. At the bottom cross two stiles to enter the field on the left, then turn left and follow the field edge, road up on the left. From here the tall chimney ahead/right is at the 'Old' Powick Bridge, **START C**, and the tree line to the right is the line of the River Teme. (For the record, this section of the walk, to **START C**, is the toughest part!, also, at certain times of the year, these fields may be flooded).

Continue following the fence line to cross a stile in the fence by a raised section of the road. Proceed in the same direction as before, across an open section, and meet the right corner of the fence ahead (**NB** do not go up the concrete track). Now continue following the left fence to reach another stile by a gate. The destination is now the tall chimney just behind the 'new' Powick Bridge, (the Teme Bridge), visible ahead. From here the correct Right of Way is to go part right, across the open meadow to meet the corner of a fence. At the fence corner turn part left and again cross the open field to pass under the left arch of the Teme Bridge, then proceed to the stile at the 'Old' Powick Bridge, **START C**.

From the Old Powick Bridge, START C: (The 'Definitive Map' of Rights of Way within the City boundary is still being prepared, however, the route used here has been in public use for many years). From a point at the old bridge, opposite the Powick Mills, cross the stiles and follow the River Teme, (on right), downstream. The route is now a gentle stroll along the River Teme and the River Severn to Worcester Bridge. The path initially follows the River Teme, over a number of stiles, and soon the tower of Worcester Cathedral comes into view over to the left.

As the river turns south, and Worcester Cathedral is to the rear, watch out for a turn left. (If you miss this you go into a loop of the River Teme and away from the path). As a guide, approx. 100 yards after the river turns south, and traffic on the A422 is visible ahead, do not cross the next stile but turn left. After only 50 yards the river bank is rejoined and this is followed to the junction with the River Severn.

As the River Teme is followed, the area to the left was the main battle-ground of the Battle of Worcester, fought on 3rd September 1651, the last battle of the English Civil War. By the junction of the rivers Teme and Severn is a City of Worcester marker stone, (and some seats), the Teme is the southern City Boundary here. At about 100 yards upstream from the river junction, on both rivers, are the sites of the boat bridges, built by the Parliamentarian forces, to convey infantry and cavalry over the river to engage, and defeat, the Royalist army of Charles II.

Now follow the River Severn upstream, (only three stiles to go to reach Worcester Bridge), on the way passing Diglis Lock and weir. It seems hard to imagine now but up to the end of the 18th century the River Severn was a major 'goods carrying highway', being navigable almost to Welshpool. Severn Trows went upstream from Gloucester using a mixture of tide, wind, man and horse power. In the mid 1800s work commenced to canalise the river up to Stourport-on-Severn, to increase the trade prospects. The advent of the railways saw the decline of the river trade.

On approaching Diglis Lock join a gravel path and follow the river bank, passing the Worcestershire County Cricket ground, and reach Worcester Bridge.   (P.K. 6/97).

The **Old Powick Bridge** *and the* **River Teme**, *(Walk 1)*.

13

Map for Walk 2   Worcester Country Park & Spetchley Park

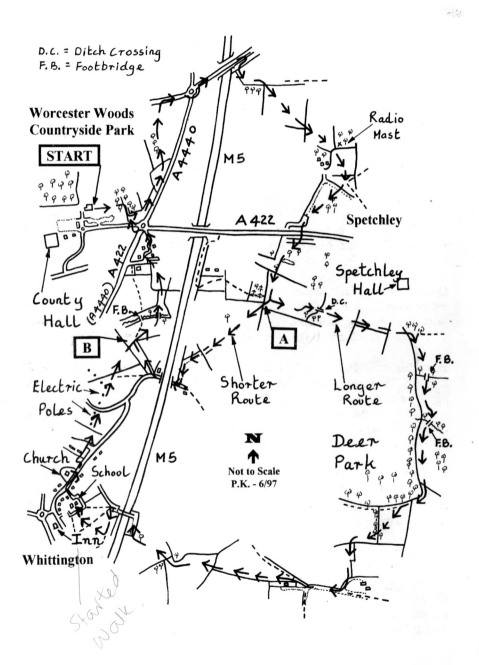

WALK 2   WORCESTER WOODS COUNTRY PARK,   3.5 or 6 Miles
SPETCHLEY PARK and WHITTINGTON

Start: The Worcester Woods Country Park, situated near County Hall, Spetchley Road, Worcester. (GR. 878544).

Parking: As above, free parking.

Refreshments: The cafe in the Visitor Centre at the Worcester Woods Country Park and, on the Longer Route, The Swan at Whittington.

O.S. Maps: Pathfinder 996 (Worcester), and Landranger 150 (Worcester & The Malverns).

Summary: A gentle walk going to the west of the M5 to Spetchley, with views to the County boundary including the Clent and Lickey Hills, Bredon Hill and the Malvern Hills. The Longer Route goes around Spetchley Park and through Whittington. Number of stiles; Shorter Route:- 9, Longer Route:- 19.

General Notes: The Worcester Woods Country Park, situated by County Hall, covers some 130 acres of woodland, open space and meadows, yet is within the City boundary. There are various waymarked routes and also a children's recreational area. This walk extends beyond the Park to explore the countryside to the east.

Route Notes: From the side entrance to the cafe at the Countryside Centre walk across the open field in an easterly direction, passing the children's play area on the right, (see map, also waymarked as the Fox Trail). Go through the tree line to a path, turn right and, after 20 yards, turn sharp left, (still the Fox Trail). Follow this horse route, trees/hedge on left, and turn left to walk parallel to the A4440. Over on the right beyond the M5 is Spetchley Park, the destination of the walk.

Ignore a stile on the left and continue parallel to the road. At the end of the field go through a bridlegate and across the field, along a slight hollow, to the right of a line of trees. At the last tree go slightly right, cross the rest of the field, go through a gate to the road and turn right. Carefully cross the dual carriageway and continue in the same direction to cross the bridge over the M5. Some 100 yards past the bridge turn sharp right onto a bridlepath and go down to the bottom of the slope.

Now go left, through a wide gate, and follow the track alongside the right hedge, (an old road to Withy Wells, pre M5). Some 50 yards past a gate in the hedge cross a stile on the right. Once over go part left across an open field, (possibly with crops), aiming for the trees to the right of a telecommunications mast.

At the top of the first field keep the same direction, via a difficult wooden gate, to proceed across another open field. (Over to the left is a good view of the Clent, Waseley and Lickey Hills, (**Walks 5**, **6** & **7**), also the Wychbold Radio Masts are visible in the middle distance.

Go through another gate and cross the field to a small gate by a tree, then go over another field to a stile by an electricity pole. Once over the stile go part right, passing to the right of the oak trees in the centre of the field, to exit the field at the far right corner, via a gate or cattle grid. Cross a stile directly ahead, go down the steps, carefully cross the A422 and go up the steps and over two stiles into a field. (Bredon Hill, **Walk 14**, and the Cotswold escarpment are ahead, the Malvern Hills, **Walk 18**, are over to the right).

Once over the second stile go part right, heading towards the trees in the far right corner of the field. Pass between a fence, (right), and a hollow, (left), a dried up pond. At the fence corner go slightly right and past a tree to cross a stile. Again head for the far right corner of the field to a gate, (in the right fence near the corner), just past the pine trees. This is **Point A** on the map, the route choice, see Page 17. (The stile into the wood is also a short route back via a path alongside the M5).

The **Worcester Countryside Centre** *at the Country Park (**Walk 2**).*

Shorter Route from Point A: Go through the iron gate, (about 30 yards to the left of the stile into the wood). Now go 45° left, across the field, keeping to the left of a lone tree, (the path should be marked through any crops). Cross a concrete bridge over a stream, go through a gate, and follow an enclosed track towards the M5. (Here a motorway sign helpfully lists two walk locations, Worcester Cathedral, **Walk 1**, and the Malvern Hills, **Walk 18**). Join a concrete path following the M5, cross a stile, (or use gate), to another track, turn right and go under the M5.

Follow this stony track past a house on the right then take the next gate on the right, a bridlepath. Go along a narrow field towards an electricity pylon to where the right hand hedge turns sharp right. This is **Point B** on the map, to complete the walk see **"Route Back to the Countryside Centre from Point B"** on Page 18.

Longer Route From Point A: For the Longer Route around Spetchley Park **do not** go through the gate but turn around and walk away from it, keeping parallel to the fence on the right. (Spetchley Hall is ahead/left). At the far end of the field keep to the left of a small group of trees, cross a stile and a ditch crossing, and then go straight across a field. (The route will usually be marked). Cross a stile, follow the fence on the right, then cross another stile.

Again go across an open field, aiming just to the right of the nearest trees ahead. Go over another stile, curve around to the right, then follow the right hedge line. Cross a footbridge hidden in the trees and after a further 200 yards cross another footbridge on the right. Now follow the right hand tree/fence line with the deer park visible beyond the fence. Go through a new bridlegate, (some nettle bashing might be necessary), and continue following the right hand tree/fence line.

Go through another bridlegate and follow the right tree line for 20 yards. Now for a minor dilemma. The Public Right of Way is to go part left, across an open field, (usually cropped), to a stile in the far hedge, (the stile is not visible but an aiming point is the centre of a row of trees on the horizon). Cross the stile, (located between two trees), and proceed across the left corner of the next field to another stile by an oak tree, some halfway along the left fence. During research there was little sign of this path being used and the use of the alternative, below, might be necessary,

If the correct Right of Way is blocked, or not marked, it is possible to proceed with the walk by continuing to follow the right tree line to the next bridlegate. Once through turn left and follow the left hedge past the stile position in that hedge, and then continue around the top of the field to the stile by the oak tree. However, this alternative is not a Right of Way and should only be used if there is a problem in following the correct route.

Cross the stile by the oak tree at the top of the **second** field, then follow the line of the left hedge as it goes towards a farmhouse, (good view of Bredon Hill ahead/left). Cross a stile to a dirt track, turn right and follow the track as it sweeps left. At a 'T' junction turn right onto bridlepath.

Keep on the gravel track for 200 yards and, as it sweeps left, take a grassy track going to the right and running parallel to a house drive. Go through a bridlegate then, after 30 yards, turn left and follow the left hedge, (the tall white building ahead in the distance is a pub!). Follow the hedge to the bottom left corner of the field, cross a stile, and keep the same direction to reach the very far right hand corner of the field, (small field inset). Cross two stiles, (one an old gate), and go part left, passing a dead tree and then up a ramp, (gate or cattle grid), to a bridge over the M5.

Once over the M5 take the gate/cattle grid on the left. From here the R of W follows the motorway for about 100 yards and then turns right, crossing the field to a stile in the fence by a school. If it is not waymarked, (the situation at the time of writing), head towards the school by the best route possible. To visit The Swan at Whittington please refer to the map, when refreshed return the same way back to the route.

If not visiting The Swan turn right on reaching the school, follow the enclosed path, school buildings on the left, to reach a road. Turn right, following the road past Whittington church, (built 1842), for 100 yards. Cross a stile on the left, turn right, follow the right hedge, cross another stile, then a farm drive, and yet another stile.

Once into the field walk to a stile by an electric pole and follow the poles, crossing a lane. Initially follow the electric poles and, as they go left, continue ahead to a stile, by a tree, in the fence. Cross and go slightly right, to a stile in a hedge, then go part left to the corner of a hedge. This is **Point B** and the link with the shorter route.

Route back to the Countryside Centre from Point B:

From the hedge corner go across the open field **almost parallel to the electric cables**, (**pylons**). Go through a metal gate to the left of an oak tree and cross a culvert bridge over a ditch. (**NB - not** the footbridge that is some 100 yards to the left of the culvert bridge). Go straight across the field to a narrow field section, go through a gate, and then proceed to another gate in the far left corner of the field.

Now cross a road, (part of the old A422), and follow the lane directly opposite which meanders around to reach the roundabout on the new A422. Carefully cross the dual carriageway to the left of the roundabout and go along Wildwood Drive for 50 yards. Now turn right and follow a bridlepath into the park for 100 yards, turn left and cross the field back to the cafe for some well-earned refreshment.   (P.K. 6/97).

18

The Junction of the **Worcs. and B'Ham Canal** *and the* **River Severn**, *(Walk 1)*.

(A contrast in modes of Transport, **18/19th** *century and* **20th** *century)*.

Footpath Bridge over the **M5**, *(Going Nowhere?)*, *(****Walk 2****)*.

19

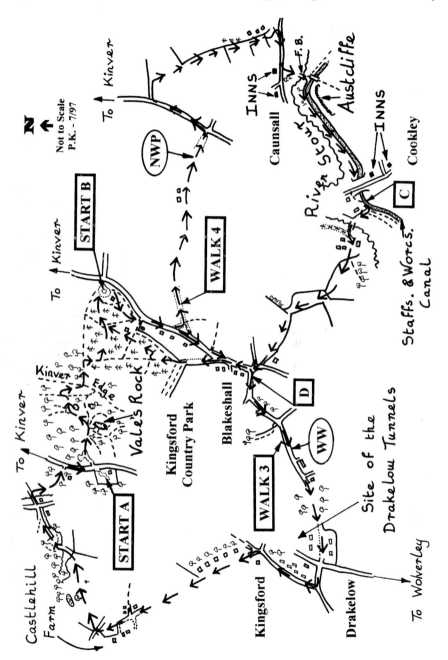

Start: The Kingsford Country Park to the north of Wolverley, from the Kingsford Lane car park, **START A** on the map,(GR. 824821), or the Blakeshall Lane car park, **START B**, at (GR. 836821).

Parking: Free parking at above car parks.

Refreshments: None at the starting points or on the route. (Picnic time?).

O.S. Maps: Pathfinder map 933 (Stourbridge & Kinver) and Landranger map 138 (Kidderminster).

Summary: A walk over Kinver Edge and then on part of the North Worcestershire Path, **(NWP)**, past the Drakelow Tunnels complex using part of the Worcestershire Way, **(WW)**, and then over Castle Hill. The start points are the Kingsford Lane car park, **START A**, (this puts the ascent of Kinver Edge at the start of the walk), or the Blakeshall Lane car park, **START B**, (which is nearer to Stourbridge). Number of stiles:- 4. This walk links with **Walk 4**, at **START B** and **Point D**, to give an overall route of 8 miles.

General Notes: Kingsford Country Park covers 200 acres of the southern end of Kinver Edge, including the sandstone outcrop of Vales Rock, both car parks have toilets. To the north is the Staffordshire part of Kinver Edge including Nanny's Rock and the recently restored, (by the National Trust), houses at Holy Austin Rock. The route does not seek to explore Kinver Edge as that can be done separately using the picnic areas and the numerous paths around this very attractive area.

Route Notes From START A: From the Kingsford Lane car park, (with the toilet block), cross the road, walk through another car park and take a sandy/stony bridlepath going gently uphill. (Here this path is the boundary between Staffordshire and Worcestershire so don't stray and get tied up in 'knots'!). This wide bridlepath route will be followed to the top of Kinver Edge as it is the easiest route.

Some 200 yards from the road ignore several paths going right and continue on the wide sandy track, (going slightly left), to eventually reach a small clearing near the base of Vale's Rock. Here the path immediately right, into the trees, goes to the remains of the rock dwellings, **(NB - dangerous)**. The small path going uphill and then sweeping right goes to the top of Vale's Rock, (good view but steep drop), and the narrower path straight ahead goes directly to the top of 'The Edge'. To continue with the route for this walk stay on the <u>wide bridlepath sweeping gently left.</u>

21

At a fork in the track, about 100 yards past Vale's Rock, keep going to the right, continuing on the bridlepath, uphill, with ample evidence of horses. At a 'T' junction turn left, after 40 yards go sharp right and then follow the track to the top of Kinver Edge. (This bridlepath strays into Staffordshire and is not as shown on the O.S. map, but please keep this fact secret). At the top, by an oak tree, is the junction of three long-distance paths, the Staffordshire Way, the North Worcestershire Path, (**NWP**), and the Worcestershire Way, (**WW**). (See notes on Page 7).

The next section of the route follows the **NWP**, (**pine cone** symbol), past **START B** to Blakeshall Lane. From the notice board follow the **NWP**, away from the 'Edge', following a line of oak trees. After about 200 yards turn right then, after 100 yards, turn left. Follow the path through the pine trees for about 250 yards to a junction of five paths. Take the second path left at the junction and follow it around to reach the notice board at the Blakeshall Lane car park. This is **START B**, an alternative starting point. (It is also a joining point for anyone adding **Walk 4** to this walk).

Route Notes from START B: From the notice board at **START B** go to the left of the toilet block following the **NWP** symbols, (**pine cone**). Cross a horse riding route and continue on the **NWP** through the wood to reach Blakeshall Lane. Turn right and follow the road, (soon leaving the **NWP** which goes off to the left), passing houses, for about 700 yards and then turn right onto a tarmac lane. (This is **Point D** on the map, a point where **Walk 4** links with this walk).

Route from Point D: From **Point D** follow the small tarmac lane going west, (wood posts on verge), and continue on it as it sweeps left. At the next junction turn right into a narrow lane and join the **WW**. From this lane the radio mast, ahead/right, is at the top of the 'Drakelow Tunnels', a series of tunnels constructed during 1941/42 as an underground factory producing aeroplane engines. From about 1960 to 1990 part of the complex was kept in readiness as a nuclear bunker.

Continue past a farm on the left and, as the road ends, keep straight ahead, on a grassy drive, past a cottage on the left. Cross a stile and follow an enclosed, sunken, track going gently downhill. (Part way down the track a path going up to the left avoids a very muddy section). As the track opens up to a rough path part of the Drakelow Tunnels compound can be seen on the right.

On reaching a road cross over and follow Sladd Lane. After 120 yards turn right, (now leaving the **WW**), onto a narrow tarmac lane and follow it for 500 yards, passing holiday bungalows on the right. At a 'T' junction keep left then take the rough track, (a bridlepath), that forks left. Follow this track, going gently uphill and passing houses on the right, towards Castlehill Farm. Near the top pass a house on the left, ignore a track going right, and pass the old Castlehill Farm over to the left.

Leave the track as it sweeps left, go ahead through a bridlegate and cross a field. Go through another bridlegate, turn right and, after 15 yards, cross a stile into a field. (To the east is Kinver Edge and beyond it are the multi-story flats at Dudley).

From the stile go part right and down the field, aiming for an isolated tree. Once past this continue over the brow of the hill and go downhill, towards Kinver Edge, to a stile between the trees near the bottom left corner of the field. Cross the stile and follow a muddy track, initially with a fence on the right, and then through trees, there are numerous horse tracks but the route is generally to the right. (Watch out for waymark posts and Staffordshire County Council yellow waymark arrows).

Go through a small open area, cross a stile and then follow the right edge of a field, (this path is a Right of Way on the Staffordshire C.C. 'Definitive Map'). The small stream down on the right is the boundary between Staffordshire and Worcestershire. At a lane, (a farm drive), turn right and at a cross-roads continue ahead. After 100 yards take a bridlepath on the right and follow this as it sweeps left to join Kingsford Lane. Here turn right and follow the road back to the car park at **START A**. (At the car park you are safely back in Worcestershire - congratulations!).

(P.K. 7/97).

The **Staffordshire** *&* **Worcestershire Canal** *at* **Austcliffe**, *(Walk 4).*

WALK 4   KINGSFORD COUNTRY PARK and COOKLEY   4.5 Miles

Start: The Kingsford Country Park north of Wolverley, from the Blakeshall Lane car park, **START B** on map, (GR. 836821).

Parking: Free parking at above.

Refreshments: At Cookley village, (Inns and shops), and two Inns at Caunsall.

O.S. Maps: Pathfinder map 933 (Stourbridge & Kinver) and Landranger maps 138 (Kidderminster) and 139 (Birmingham).

Summary: A walk along parts of the North Worcestershire Path, (**NWP**), and the Staffordshire and Worcestershire Canal. (It could be started from Cookley village but there are parking restrictions, **Point C** on the map is the link point). Number of stiles:- 8. This walk links with **Walk 3** at the start point, and at **Point D**, to give a walk of 8 miles. The **Route Map** for this walk is on **Page 20**.

General Notes: See the notes in **Walk 3** regarding the Kingsford Country Park. This is a gentle walk with a choice of four pubs for a break, just relax and enjoy it!.

Route Notes From START B: (**START A** is used for **Walk 3** which is on the same map as **Walk 4**). From the notice board at the Blakeshall Lane car park go to the left of the toilet block and follow the **NWP**, (pine cone symbols). Cross a horse riding route and continue through the wood to Blakeshall Lane, turn right, along the lane, for 150 yards and take a footpath going off to the left, the **NWP**.

Follow the footpath and at a path junction, (after about 100 yards), turn left. Now follow this bridlepath, (still the **NWP**), gently downhill, (ahead/right are the **Clent, Waseley** and **Lickey Hills, Walks 5, 6** and **7**), to reach a road, (Kinver Lane), here turn left. Follow the road for 500 yards and then cross a stile, on the right, into a field. Follow the left hedge for just over 100 yards, turn right, first following a wide path across the centre of the field and then a fence/hedge on the left.

Cross a stile by a gate, follow a line of trees on the left and cross two more stiles. Pass farm buildings on the left, then join a gravel track that sweeps around to a stile onto a road. Here turn right and follow the road, (leaving the **NWP**), for some 300 yards through the village of Caunsall, to a path on the left. (**NB** just along the road from this point are two Inns!). Take the path going left, (or on the right if returning from the pub!), via a gate, (old kissing gate partly hidden in the hedge). Follow the path to cross the River Stour and reach the towpath of the Staffs. & Worcs. Canal.

The Staffordshire and Worcestershire Canal was constructed by James Brindley and opened in 1772, linking the Trent and Mersey Canal at Great Haywood with the River Severn at Stourport-on-Severn. The canal is 46 miles long with 45 locks. In most instances, as here, canal towpaths are not Public Rights of Way, but British Waterways allow the use of them for recreational purposes such as walking.

At the canal, by Bridge No. 24, turn right, (the sandstone face of Austcliffe now on your left), and follow the towpath, (the River Stour down on the right), to reach and pass through Cookley Tunnel, (65 yards long). Some 50 yards beyond the tunnel the path on the right, (**Point C**), goes up to Cookley Village, some 200 yards away. To continue the walk, follow the towpath to pass over an iron bridge about 200 yards past the tunnel, (old canal arm to a factory), and cross a stile on the right. Follow the path alongside the factory wall, (on right), again cross the River Stour and at a 'T' junction turn left.

Follow the wide track as it goes right and left, passing farm buildings on the left and corrugated iron barns on the right. Go through a gate into a field and take the path to the right that follows the bottom of a small valley. At the far end cross a stile, (poor condition in June 1997), and go across a small section of open field, (about 50 yards), to the corner of a fence. Follow the fence, (on left), up a narrow field and continue to follow it as it sweeps left and right, (passing farm buildings), to cross a stile to a road. Here go right, pass a road junction, (on right), and reach a narrow lane going left. This is **Point D** on the map and a link with **Walk 3**. (Anyone wishing to add **Walk 3** to this walk should turn left into the narrow lane and refer to the notes in **Walk 3**. Those people wishing to finish **Walk 4** continue as below).

Route from Point D: From **Point D** continue following the road you are already on, heading back to **START B**. After some 250 yards, turn part left onto a dirt track, just past Cedar Lodge, and follow this, passing a field on the left. Now keep the same direction, (ignore two parallel tracks going left), and continue ahead to a point 50 yards past the end of the field. Leave the horse riding route by a narrow path forking left which soon opens up to a wider track through the pine wood.

At a path cross-roads turn right then, after 20 yards, turn left onto a narrow path. Follow this path through the pines and cross over the next junction, a shed and timber yard on the right. Proceed to the next junction of five wide paths, cross over and take the path going ahead/right, (back on the **NWP**). Follow this track as it curves right to reach the Blakeshall Lane car park, **START B** on map. (P.K. 6/97)

Map for Walk 5

Clent Hills and Uffmoor Wood

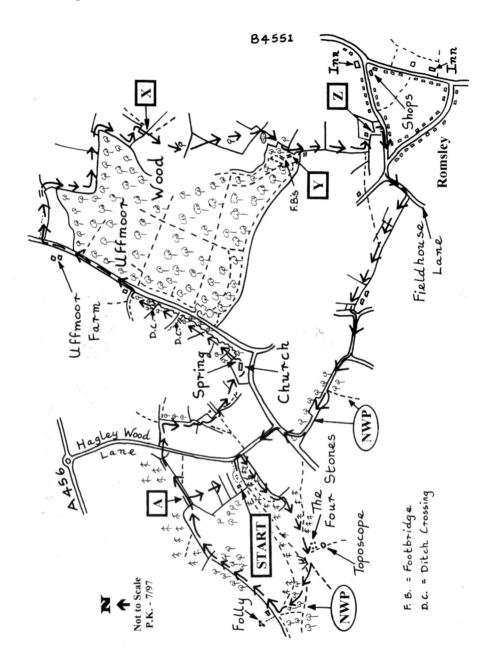

B4551

X

Z

Inn

Inn

Shops

Romsley

Y

F.B.'s

Uffmoor Wood

Fieldhouse Lane

Uffmoor Farm

D.C.

D.C.

Spring

Church

NWP

Hagley Wood Lane

A456

A

The Four Stones

START

Toposcope

NWP

Folly

N

Not to Scale
P.K. - 7/97

F. B. = Footbridge
D.C. = Ditch Crossing

WALK 5 **CLENT HILLS and UFFMOOR WOOD** **1.5 or 6 Miles**

Start: The Nimmings Car Park and Visitor Centre, off Hagley Wood Lane, at the north-east of the Clent Hills. (GR. 938807).

Parking: At the Visitor Centre, parking charge.

Refreshments: Kiosk at the Visitor Centre, open every day except Xmas Day. None on route but a short detour visits pubs/shops in Romsley.

O.S. Maps: Pathfinder maps 933 (Stourbridge), and 953 (Kidderminster). Also Landranger map 139 (Birmingham).

Summary: A walk to the main viewpoint of the Clent Hills to look across Worcestershire and then around Uffmoor Wood, which is on the County boundary, returning via Romsley. The 'Shorter Walk' is just the visit to the viewpoint. This walk links with **Walk 6** at **Points X** and **Z**. For people doing the longer walk only there is an alternative car park, and starting point, (when open), at **Point Z**, (see notes on Page 30). Number of stiles; Shorter Route:- 2, Longer Route:- 25.

General Notes: The Clent Hills, the 'country playground' of people from 'The Black Country' and Birmingham, are a series of hills near the village of Clent. The area offers many walking opportunities, (on Public Rights of Way and permissive paths), on land owned mainly by the National Trust and partly by the County Council. The overall area can be explored, at leisure, separately from this book.

Route Notes: From the car park walk back to the entrance, turn right for 40 yards, then go right again, past a wood barrier, and walk up the hill. (This route is not the shortest to the viewpoint but offers a view over Romsley and the Longer Route). Follow the path uphill keeping the fence on the left in view, (several paths), and, as the path levels out, go through a wood barrier on the left, leaving the wood.

From here the route is right, to initially follow the fence on the right, but first look north-east. The large expanse of woodland in the valley below is Uffmoor Wood, the Longer Route goes around its northern boundary, and over to the right is Romsley village. To continue the walk, initially follow the fence on the right, then a wide track, joining the North Worcestershire Path, (**NWP**, pine cone symbol, see notes on Page 7), to reach the 'Four Stones' and also the viewpoint, (the toposcope).

The 'Four Stones' is a 'folly' erected by the owners of Hagley Hall. The Rotary Club toposcope shows the places visible from this 997 ft. summit, across a large part of Worcestershire, including Bredon Hill and The Malvern Hills.

27

To continue on the route follow the **NWP** going west, (i.e. if walking back to the 'Stones' from the toposcope, go left). After 100 yards take the track forking right to reach the 'AA' viewpoint, (views over Shropshire and The Black Country). Continue on the grassy path going downhill into the trees, (still **NWP**), and about 150 yards past the 'AA' viewpoint take another right fork, leaving the **NWP**, and going downhill towards the 'ruined castle' folly. Enter trees and, at a 'T' junction, turn left and after 50 yards, with the folly ahead, turn right.

Now follow the wide gravel track and, as it sweeps left, keep straight ahead entering a field. Follow the left tree line for 200 yards then go slightly right to a stile by a gate. Here the next stile on the right is **Point A**. For the shorter route cross the stile, going over the field and through three kissing gates, to reach the Visitor Centre.

For the longer route **do not** cross the stile on the right but follow the wide track, trees on left, to cross Hagley Wood Lane and a stile to a field. Follow the left hedge/tree line to within 10 yards of the far left corner and turn right, (i.e. **do not** cross the stiles). Again follow the left hedge and at the top left corner cross the stile to the right, cross another stile after 10 yards and turn right. Walk into the field for 50 yards and then turn left, first across an open part of the field and then alongside a hedge on the left, ruined cottage beyond. At a track go left and, almost immediately turn right and cross a stile.

St Kenelm's Church *(Walk 5)*.

28

The **Holy Spring** *at* **St. Kenelm's Church**, *(Walk 5).*

Now cross the field to a gap in the old hedgerow, (NB. not the track near the right hedge). Proceed to a stile and then to St. Kenelm's Church and the spring beyond it. The church is of Norman origin and dedicated to Kenelm, the young King of Mercia, who, legend has it, was murdered in 819 and his body found at this location.

The spring here was supposed to have miraculous powers, particularly healing sore eyes, (those who try it today may well need a miraculous faith in the NHS to restore them to health and strength). It is, however, a delightful place to rest awhile. The spring, and the area around it, have been restored and landscaped with funds provided by the North Worcestershire Countryside Action Project, (NWCAP).

From the spring area follow the well-defined path away from the church, a small stream down on the right. The path passes through fields and woodland, generally following the line of the stream, passing over 5 stiles and 2 ditch crossings, to reach a drive. Here turn right, go through a gate to a road, and turn left. On the opposite side of the road from the drive is one of the entrances to Uffmoor Wood, 212 acres of part semi-natural ancient woodland, owned by The Woodland Trust, and normally open to the public. There are no Public Rights of Way in the wood but NWCAP have negotiated, and installed, a permissive path at **Point Y**, (see Page 30), allowing access between the wood and the adjacent Public Footpath network.

Follow the road northwards, to 100 yards past the buildings of Uffmoor Farm, and then turn right up a farm drive. (Watch for fast traffic on this 700 yard stretch of road, the author suspects that drivers are awarded bonus points for hitting ramblers!. Also, having crossed the County boundary, you are now in Dudley M.B.C. territory).

Follow the drive over a bridge, cross a stile and turn right to follow the right field edge. The route from here to near Romsley is well marked with yellow topped posts. Continue along the edge of Uffmoor Wood, crossing two stiles and turning right. About 200 yards after turning right curve left, **away** from the wood. Follow the right hedge/fence to a stile in the far right corner, cross this and then another stile immediately ahead. This is **Point X**, a link with **Walk 6**. (From here to **Point Z** the route is as **Walk 6** but in the opposite direction).

Now go slightly right, crossing the field, towards a large isolated tree in the hedge ahead. Cross the stile by the tree, (you are back in Worcestershire), go 45° left, cross the field corner and go through a narrow stile. Now go 45° right, across an open field, (passing an isolated tree), to another narrow stile in the far left corner of the field. Follow the right side of the field, past a fishing pond, crossing a stile into the trees. Follow the left fence and cross a stile, this is **Point Y**, the steps going down to the right, and across two footbridges, is the permissive path into Uffmoor Wood.

To continue with this route go up the steps on the left, turn to the right and follow the right hedge. Proceed, via another stile, to the far right corner of a field and turn left, (ignoring a stile on the right). Cross another stile to reach a hut and playing field and turn right to a parking area, this is **Point Z**, the other link with **Walk 6** and the alternative parking area. This site has been provided, to give access to the countryside, with funds from NWCAP, and is administered by Romsley Parish Council. From the entrance the road left leads to a pub and shops, (see map).

The route to the Nimmings Car Park and the Clent Hills is now out of this car park, turn right along the road for 500 yards, then turn left into Fieldhouse Lane. Follow the lane for 200 yards and take the footpath on the right signposted Walton Hill, continuing along the left hedge, over stiles, to reach a road.

At the road turn left and, at an immediate 'T' junction, turn right. Follow the road, to another 'T' junction, turn right, (now joining the **NWP** again), pass a parking area and at the next 'T' junction turn right again, (now leaving the **NWP**). After 150 yards turn left into Hagley Wood Lane and return to the Visitor Centre. (**NB** people starting from **Point Z** should take the path going left some 40 yards before the entrance to Nimmings Car Park, unless visiting the cafe). (P.K. 7/97).

The **Visitor Centre** *at the* **Waseley Hills Country Park,** *(Walks 6 & 7).*

The **Worcester and Birmingham Canal** *at* **Tardebigge,** *(Walk 8).*

Map for Walk 6   Romsley from Waseley Hills Country Park

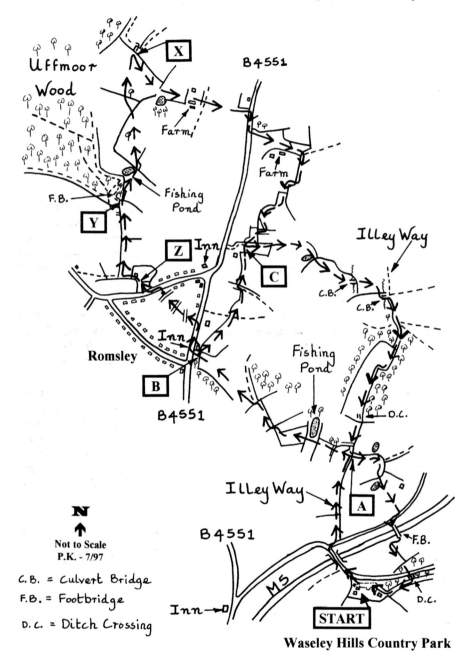

Uffmoor Wood

X

B4551

Farm

Farm

F.B.

Fishing Pond

Y

Z Inn

C

Illey Way

C.B.

C.B.

Inn

Romsley

Fishing Pond

D.C.

B

B4551

Illey Way

A

N

↑

Not to Scale
P.K. - 7/97

C.B. = Culvert Bridge

F.B. = Footbridge

D.C. = Ditch Crossing

B4551

F.B.

M5

Inn →

D.C.

START

Waseley Hills Country Park

WALK 6 **Around ROMSLEY from the** **1.5, 4 or 5.5 Miles**
WASELEY HILLS COUNTRY PARK

Start: The Visitor Centre and cafe at the North Car Park of the Waseley Hills Country Park, (near the B4551). (GR. 972782).

Parking: At the Visitor Centre, parking charge.

Refreshments: Cafe at the Visitor Centre, Pubs and shops in Romsley.

O.S. Maps: Pathfinder maps 933 (Stourbridge), and 953 (Kidderminster). Also Landranger map 139 (Birmingham).

Summary: A walk north of the Waseley Hills Country Park offering a range of route lengths. A 1.5 mile stroll, a medium route of 4 miles or a longer route of 5.5 miles that also links with **Walk 5** at **Points Z** and **X** on the map. The longer route also passes the permissive path into Uffmoor Wood at **Point Y**, (more easily located from this walk than coming through the Wood). For people doing the longer route there is an alternative starting point, (when open), at **Point Z**. Number of stiles; Short Route:- 10, Medium Route:- 22, Longer Route:- 33.

General Notes: The Waseley Hills County Park comprises 150 acres of grassy hills with self guided trails, orienteering course and running trail. This route visits Public Rights of Way north of the park and includes a small section of the Illey Way, a 4.5 mile route linking the Waseley Hills and the Woodgate Valley Country Parks.

Route Notes: From the car park return to the road and turn left, going over the M5. Go right into Newton Lane and after 100 yards cross a stile on the left. Now follow the Illey Way, hedge on right, (view towards Dudley), going over another stile, to reach a stile on the right 50 yards before the field corner; **(Point A)**. For the Short Stroll cross the stile on the right then turn to Page 35 and the heading, **"Route Back from Point A"**. For the Medium or Longer Route **do not** use this stile but turn full left, leaving the Illey Way, and cross the middle of the open field towards the largest tree in the hedge ahead.

Cross two stiles by the tree, follow right hedge, go over another stile and past a fishing pond to the right. Enter the next field, go part right and up to the top corner, use a stile, (or gate), and follow the left tree line. At the next gateway cross a stile to its left and continue ahead, fence on the right. Cross a stile 50 yards to the left of the far right corner and go straight across the open field. (The roof of The Fighting Cocks Inn visible beyond the trees). Once across the field go around, (or over!), the stile and reach **Point B**. See next page for a choice of routes, (Medium or Long).

33

Medium Route from Point B: Having gone around the stile at **Point B** do not go to the pub, (OK, a quick one if you must!), but turn right, go through a gate and follow the left hedge. The route now passes a cricket ground and several fields, (no stiles), with a view, right, of the M5 'rat race'. At the solid hedge ahead turn left for 10 yards then go right and around a stile. Again follow the left hedge, passing Porch House Farm, (on the left), then over a stile and cross a small field. **Do not** use the stile or the gap ahead but turn right, this is **Point C** on the map. To finish the walk see Page 35 and the heading, **"Route Back (Point C to Point A)"**.

Longer Route from Point B: Go past the Inn (!) to the road, turning right, to a point just past St. Kenelm's C of E School. (Another Inn and shops are further down the road). Turn left, carefully cross the road and take an enclosed path between houses, going over three estate roads and past garages, to another main road. Here turn left and after 50 yards turn right into a car park, **Point Z** on map, a link with **Walk 5**. (An alternative starting point, (free), for people doing the Longer Walk). This car park was funded by the North Worcestershire Countryside Action Project, (NWCAP), and is administered by Romsley Parish Council.

From the car park at **Point Z** take the path alongside the playing field and turn left before the hut. Cross a stile and, at the field corner, ignore the stile ahead and turn right. Continue following the left hedge, (view towards Dudley), crossing one stile then going down steps to stile in the trees. This is **Point Y** on the map, a permissive path, (negotiated and installed by NWCAP), goes to Uffmoor Wood via the steps going down to the left, then over two footbridges. (Also a possible link with **Walk 5**, for details of the Uffmoor Wood permissive paths see the notes and map in **Walk 5**).

For **Walk 6** ignore the steps going down to the footbridges and cross the stile ahead, pass through trees and enter a field. Pass a fishing pool, (on the left), go through a stile and turn left along a track for 50 yards. Now go part right, across an open field, passing marker posts and a large tree, then through stile in the far left hedge. Cross the corner of a field to a stile by a large tree, (County boundary), and go straight across the field to reach a stile by a gate, **Point X**, another link with **Walk 5**.

Do not cross the stile ahead but turn right, generally follow the left fence/hedge, then join a track, (now back in Worcestershire), heading towards farm buildings. (NB the route keeps to Public Rights of Way). Near the farm buildings cross a stile, pass the barns, (on the right), and follow the track to the B4551.

At the road turn right and after 200 yards, by a slight bend, CAREFULLY cross the road and go over a stile into a field. Cross the open field aiming to the left of the farm buildings ahead. Pass the barns, (on right), keeping the same direction to cross a stile by a metal gate.

Now follow a track with a fence, (then a hedge), on the right and **near the end** of the hedge cross a stile on the right. Follow the left hedge as it turns left, cross a stile then, at the end of the hedge, turn right. Cross a small section of field then follow the right fence/hedge as it curves left.

Cross a stile to a track, turn right, and after 25 yards cross two stiles on the left, (by gates). Go diagonally left over a small field, joining a stony track to a stile on the left, by a gap in the hedge. Once through the gap turn left, this is **Point C** on the map, the link point with the Medium Walk. To continue the walk see below.

Route Back (Point C to Point A): Follow the left hedge, cross a stile and join a wide track with the M5 ahead. At a pond turn right, once past a gate go part left crossing the end of a field, to reach a culvert bridge prior to a stile and gate. Now go across an open field, similar direction as before, to the **very far** right corner of the field. Cross the stile in the corner, (hidden until you reach it), turn left over another culvert bridge, and immediately turn right, rejoining the Illey Way, (and also **The Monarch's Way**, see Page 7), but in the opposite direction to the start of the walk.

Keep on this wide track, the Illey Way, ignoring all other paths off it, and pass through woodland to reach an open field. Use the stile or gate into the field, turn left, and follow the left tree line. Go over a ditch crossing and a stile, continue along the left hedge, cross two stiles close together, then turn left. Cross the corner of the field and this time cross the stile on the left, leaving the Illey Way, to reach **Point A**.

Route Back from Point A: Having crossed the stile turn left and follow the left hedge, passing a pond and a stile to reach the fence at the top of the field. (The path around the side of the field is a Right of Way, there is no official path across the field). On reaching the top fence follow it to a point just past the house over to the left and then cross a stile on the left. Go past a pond on the right and then turn part right, walking toward an electricity pylon. Cross a stile to a road and turn right.

Continue along the road for about 200 yards to a stile on the left, partly hidden by trees. Now follow the path to a footbridge over the M5 and then turn right. After some 50 yards following the right hand fence turn left and take the path that keeps the hedge on the **left**. Cross a difficult stile into a wood then CAREFULLY cross a road, going over a ditch crossing to reach a track. Here turn right, (now back in the Waseley Hills Country Park), and follow the track, as it sweeps to the right, to return to the Visitor Centre, car park and cafe.   (P.K. 7/97).

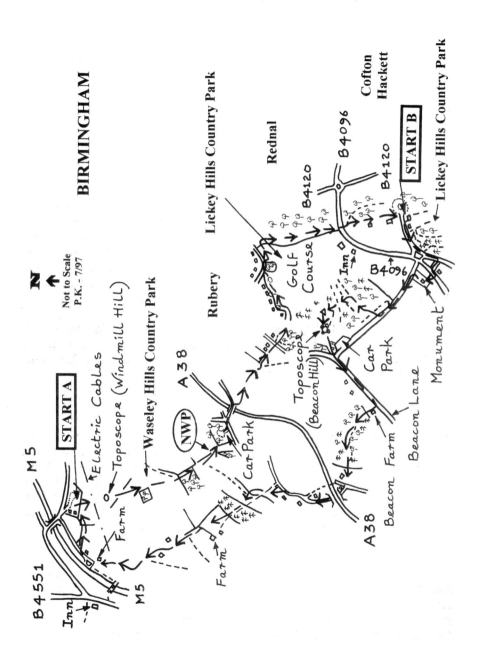

WALK 7	The WASELEY HILLS and	7 Miles
	LICKEY HILLS Circular	

Start: The Visitor Centres, Waseley Hills, (**START A**, GR. 972782), & Lickey Hills, (**START B**, GR. 997754), of the Country Parks.

Parking: At both Visitor Centres, (parking charge at Waseley Hills).

Refreshments: Cafe at both Visitor Centres, none directly on the route.

O.S. Maps: Pathfinder map 953 (Kidderminster), and Landranger map 139 (Birmingham).

Summary: A walk linking the Visitor Centres of both Country Parks, (the alternative Start Points), also the high points, Windmill Hill and Beacon Hill, and including a section of the North Worcestershire Path, (**NWP**). (Chose a clear day to enjoy the panoramic views over Worcestershire, the Black Country and Birmingham). It is also possible to start the walk from the Waseley Hills South Car Park, or the Lickey Hills Beacon Hill Car Park, both passed on the walk, however, details are not included in the Route Notes. Number of stiles:- 8.

General Notes: The Lickey Hills Country Park, which is in Worcestershire, is owned and administered by the City of Birmingham. It comprises 524 acres of woodland and open space, including the Municipal Golf Course of Rose Hill. Brief details of the Waseley Hills Country Park are given in **Walk 6.**

Route Notes:

Waseley to Lickey, (START A): From the visitor centre go past the notice boards, through the kissing gate, (KG), and straight up the hill. Ascend some steps to reach the toposcope on Windmill Hill and enjoy the panoramic view, the Lickey Hills, the destination of this walk, are to the south east. From the toposcope head towards the Lickey Hills, (you can cheat by using the toposcope instead of a compass). Follow the crest of the hill and soon encounter a signpost with the pine cone symbol of the **NWP**, (followed for part of this route). Go through a wide gap in the double fencing and head towards the left edge of the small wood ahead.

Proceed gently downhill, through a KG, and follow a wide track, hedge on the left. Pass through another KG and keep the same direction, following a line of trees on the left. Eventually take a path that goes downhill, to the left and over a field, to a gate. Go through another KG and follow the path as it sweeps right and left, (several variations), to reach the South Car Park of the Waseley Hills Country Park.

Go to the road, turn left for 100 yards, then turn right using the road bridge over the A38. Once over the bridge turn right onto a bridlepath and follow this stony track as it goes left and then meanders through the countryside. Some 500 yards beyond the road look for a footpath going left. Leave the bridlepath, going into a field, and follow the path as it sweeps gently right, a wire mesh fence now on the left. Pass houses on the left, cross a stile and then a road, and continue along the right hand tarmac drive on the opposite side, (now **leaving** the **NWP**).

At the end of the tarmac drive continue ahead to reach the Rose Hill Golf Course, (a City of Birmingham Municipal Golf Course). Here turn left and follow the left edge of the Golf Course. The route now goes around the edge of the Golf Course, initially on a Right of Way but then on a path frequently used by the public. However, the Golf Course is part of the Lickey Hills Country Park and walkers have access to it providing they do not interfere with play, (but do watch out for airborne golf balls!).

Now keep to the left edge of the Course, ignoring paths going left, to reach a 'green' in the far left hand corner. Here go left, via a KG, to a road and turn right. Follow the road for about 100 yards, (now in Birmingham), turn right again, back onto the Golf Course, and go to the left. Follow the left edge of the Course, cross a stile ahead and turn right. Follow a muddy track, Golf Course on the right, to eventually reach the B4096, (now back in Worcestershire). CAREFULLY cross the road and take the bridlepath opposite/left, rejoining the **NWP**. Keep on this track, ignoring steps to the left, and reach the Visitor Centre of the Lickey Hills Country Park.

Lickey to Waseley, (START B):   On leaving the front entrance to the Visitor Centre turn left along the road. At a fork in the road keep left and at the 'T' junction turn left. (There are paths through the wood but they are numerous and difficult to describe accurately). Go along the road for about 100 yards, turn right and go through the cemetery. At the B4096 turn left for some 50 yards, turn right, CAREFULLY cross the road, and take a path through the trees. Proceed to the obelisk commemorating the Sixth Earl of Plymouth, (Other Archer), and the Worcestershire Yeomanry Cavalry. (The rest you can read for yourself!).

At the obelisk turn right along the wide grassed area and reach the aptly named Monument Lane, turn left and follow the road for 600 yards. By No. 61 turn right, crossing the road, and then following the wide path back into the Country Park. Follow this wide path, ignoring numerous paths off it, for some 300 yards, then go up the steps on the left. At the top continue straight ahead, ignoring many intersecting paths, to reach an O.S. Trig. Point, (now redundant). Now turn left, follow the left edge of the open grass area, and reach the mock castle and viewpoint at the top of Beacon Hill. (This folly was erected to commemorate the gift of Beacon Hill to the City of Birmingham, by the Cadbury Brothers, in 1907).

The **Clent** *and* **Waseley Hills** *from* **Beacon Hill**, *(Walk 7).*

Having seen the view continue past the folly, same direction as before, on a track close to the right tree line, (car park over on the left). At the road, (Beacon Hill), turn left and join Beacon Lane, following it for 550 yards. At Beacon Farm turn right onto a bridlepath, passing farm buildings, to a path through woodland. Go gently downhill on the muddy path, (small path on left avoids most of the mud), then go through a metal gate and past a house. Follow the drive to a road and turn left.

Follow the old road to a barrier, turn right under the A38, then along a meandering road for some 800 yards, (watch out for traffic). (A footpath across the A38, (!*!), is only suitable for people having a death wish). Some 25 yards past cottages, (on left), cross a stile on the left. Head across the field, (slightly right), go over a farm drive, then follow the left hedge going gently uphill. After 150 yards go through a KG on the left and across the field to a stile, about 10 yards to the right of the farm drive.

Follow the path through the trees, cross a stile to a field, (very boggy here), and proceed up the field to the diagonally opposite corner. Cross a stile onto a wide bridlepath and follow it, through kissing gates, for some 1000 yards to reach farm buildings. Take the tarmac road that forks right, (joining the **NWP**), follow it for 330 yards, then turn right onto a footpath some 40 yards past a cottage. Follow the footpath, fence/hedge on the left, cross two stiles close together, then turn left and reach the Visitor Centre and cafe at the Waseley Hills Country Park. (P.K. 7/97).

39

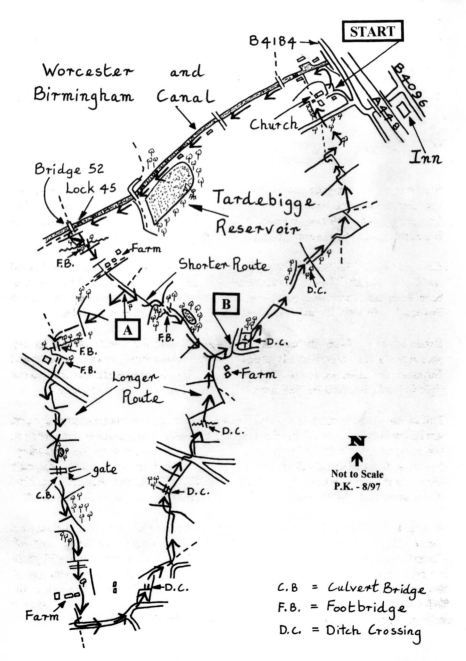

START

B4184 →

B4096

A448

Worcester and Canal
Birmingham Canal

Church

Inn

Bridge 52
Lock 45

Tardebigge
Reservoir

F.B.

Farm

Shorter Route

D.C.

A

B

F.B.

D.C.

F.B.
F.B.

Longer
Route

Farm

D.C.

N
↑
Not to Scale
P.K. - 8/97

gate

C.B.

D.C.

D.C.

Farm

C.B. = Culvert Bridge
F.B. = Footbridge
D.C. = Ditch Crossing

40

Walk 8   **TARDEBIGGE, the RESERVOIR,**   **3 or 5.5 Miles**
                the CANAL and the COUNTRYSIDE

Start: The car park by Tardebigge church, off B4184. (GR. 996692).

Parking: At the above car park, no charge.

Refreshments: None on the route but 'The Tardebigge', (an inn), is close to the
                start point on the B4096, (go under the A448).

O.S. Maps: Pathfinder map 974 (Droitwich). Also Landranger maps 139
                (Birmingham) and 150 (Worcester and The Malverns).

Summary: A walk along part of the Worcester and Birmingham Canal, past
Tardebigge Reservoir, into the countryside and crossing several cultivated fields.
This walk is anti-clockwise to go down the canal and, on the return, the church spire
is a useful guide. Number of stiles; Shorter Route:- 16, Longer Route:- 37.

General Notes: The start point is the car park, which is administered by Tutnall
and Cobley Parish Council, for the Tardebigge church and school. It has, however,
been landscaped and improved by the North Worcestershire Countryside Action
Programme, (NWCAP), and is thus available for use by the general public.

Route Notes: From the car park, with your back to the church, use the kissing
gate at the far left corner and take the path, (steps and handrail), to the Worcester and
Birmingham Canal, (see notes in **Walk 1**, Page 11). At the towpath turn left, (to the
right is Tardebigge Tunnel, 580 yards long, one of five tunnels on the canal).

Follow the towpath down the canal, (generally towpaths are permissive paths and
not Rights of Way). Pass Tardebigge Top Lock, (useful information board), the first,
(or last), of a flight of 30 locks over 2.5 miles, and continue to the Tardebigge
Reservoir, (on the left). (A short detour to the rim of the reservoir is worthwhile, with
views across Worcestershire to the Malvern Hills, **Walk 18**, and also to Shropshire.
The reservoir was built, along with others, to supply 'top up' water for the canal).

Having seen the reservoir, and the view, return to the towpath and continue down the
canal. Go past lock 45, under bridge 52, then 20 yards past the bridge turn left
through the trees and over a stile. Go down the field to a footbridge some 30 yards
from the bottom right corner, then up the bank and across a field to the right end of
the farm buildings. Go through two metal gates, farm track between, and follow the
left hedge for 75 yards to a stile on the left. This is **Point A** on the map, yet again it
is decision time, 3 miles or 5.5 miles? Having decided see the next page.

41

Shorter Route, from Point A: Do not cross the stile on the left but continue to follow the left hedge and, at the far left corner, cross a difficult stile on the left. (This shorter route was not in regular use when researched in August 1997). Having successfully negotiated the stile follow the right edge of the field for 50 yards and turn right, into an overgrown clearing between trees. Proceed to the far end, (it could be a nettle bashing time!), go over a stile, then a footbridge, and enter a field. Keep the same general direction, following the left hedge and passing a pond. Cross a stile by an old metal gate and eventually reach another old metal gate in the far left corner of the field. Go through, turn 45° right, and cross the corner of the field to a gate to a road. This is **Point B** on the map, to finish the walk see Page 43.

Longer Route, from Point A: With your back to the fence/hedge, (and the stile), go across the open field, (no aiming point), to a stile in the far fence, (visible when part way across the field). Now go part right across the corner of a field and over another stile, keeping the same direction. Cross a footbridge in the left tree line some 100 yards from the far left corner of the field. (NB, far side of the footbridge can be boggy). Go around the trees, (by the least boggy route you can find!), and follow the fence line on the right. Cross another stile and a footbridge, (Tardebigge Farm to the right), and cross the bottom of a garden to a stile to the road.

CAREFULLY cross the road, go up steps and over the stile, then turn left. Follow the left hedge for about 100 yards, go through a gap on the left, then continue in the same direction as before, hedge now on the right. Go over a stile in the hedge ahead, pass a small pond, (on left), and reach two makeshift stiles, either side of a culvert bridge. (If the stiles prove difficult there is a gate some 50 yards to the left).

Once past the culvert bridge go straight across the field to the far corner, (stile or gate), then turn left. Follow the left hedge, over another stile, and continue following the left hedge for about 100 yards. Now go gently uphill and to the right to join the right tree line. Follow this to the very far right corner to cross three stiles fairly close together. In the next field go generally to the right, passing a large oak tree, then farm buildings, to reach the far right corner. Go over a stile to reach the road and turn left.

Follow the road for about 400 yards, passing a turn off to the right, to where the road bends right. Here cross a stile on left, (close to a gate). Once over go part right to a stile and ditch crossing in the opposite hedge. Proceed to the top right corner of the field, go through a gate and follow the left hedge. At the top corner cross a stile and turn left, following the left hedge for 300 yards to a gate at the far left corner of the field. Once through turn right, cross the stile ahead and generally follow the right hedge, (Tardebigge church spire visible ahead/right), crossing a total of four stiles and a ditch crossing to reach a road. Here turn right.

42

Follow the road for 50 yards, (ignore turn off to the right), and go through a gate on the left. Follow the right hedge for 100 yards, cross a stile on the right, then go part left, across the end of the field, aiming for the trees on the opposite side. Go over a ditch crossing, turn 45° right, and reach a stile in a fence. Continue in the same general direction to a stile in the **top** right corner of the field, (ignore the stile in the hedge to the right). Once over the stile follow the right hedge, (farm to the right), go through a gate, then 45° right, crossing the corner of the field to a gate to a road. This is **Point B** on the map, to continue the walk see below.

Route Back from Point B:

At the road turn left for 30 yards, then cross the road and go through a gate into a small field. Cross the field, via a ditch crossing, to the far left corner, cross a stile and turn left. Follow the edge of the field, initially with trees to the left, for about 250 yards. Now cross two stiles on the left and go straight across an open section of a field, aiming for the nearest tree. Keep the tree and a drainage channel to the left and, after about 50 yards, go slightly right, across another section of open field, to follow the left side of a row of trees. Cross a ditch crossing and stile, then follow the right hedge for 400 yards to reach a gate on the right, an intersection of two paths.

On reaching the gate turn left, (i.e. **do not** go through the gate), crossing the corner of the field to a gate in the far hedge, (about 100 yards from the far right corner of the field). The route here joins The **Monarch's Way**, a 610 mile path, covered in three books, researched and written by Trevor Antill, (published by Meridian Books, see also the notes on Page 7). Go through the gate, follow the left hedge for 50 yards, go through a gap/gate on the left, and cross the field aiming for a gate to the left of Tardebigge Church spire. Once through the gate go around the right side of the field to a hidden stile, some 20 yards left of the far right corner.

Cross the stile and initially follow the right hedge, then cross the open field to an isolated tree. Now turn 90 left, crossing the open field to a stile to the road. (This is the correct Right of Way and follows the old hedge line, the tempting alternative diagonally over the field is not an official footpath). Cross the road, then follow the left hedge past a school playground to the churchyard. Here turn right and go past the church to the car park. (The route through the churchyard back to the car park is not an official Right of Way, but it is in frequent use by people visiting the church. St Bartholomew's Church, with its distinctive spire that is visible for miles around, was built in 1777). (P.K. 8/97).

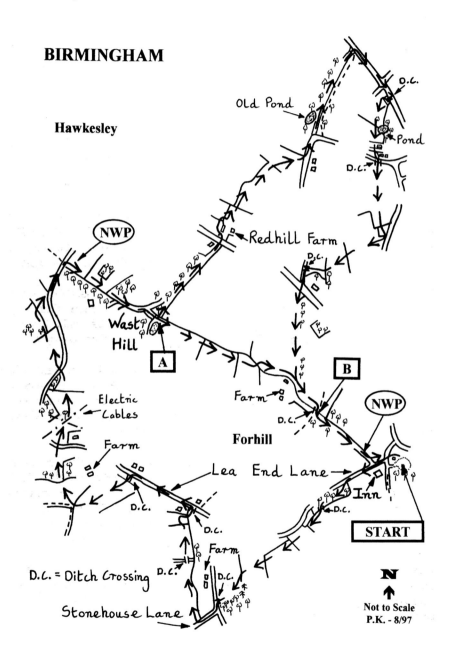

BIRMINGHAM

Hawkesley

Old Pond

O.C.

Pond

D.C.

NWP

Redhill Farm

D.C.

Wast Hill

A

B

Electric Cables

Farm

NWP

Farm

Forhill

D.C.

Lea End Lane

Farm

Inn

D.C.

D.C.

START

D.C.

Farm

D.C. = Ditch Crossing

D.C.

D.C.

Stonehouse Lane

N

↑

Not to Scale
P.K. - 8/97

44

WALK 9   **FORHILL and WAST HILL**   **4 or 6 Miles**

Start: The County Council Picnic Place at Forhill. (GR. 055755).

Parking: At the Worcestershire County Council Picnic Place, as above.

Refreshments: 'The Peacock' by the Picnic Place, none on the route.

O.S. Maps: Pathfinder 954 (Solihull), and Landranger 139 (Birmingham).

Summary: A walk near the County Boundary with Birmingham using sections of The Icknield Way, the **North Worcestershire Path, (NWP)**, and going over Wast Hill. This walk can be linked with **Walk 10** to make a variable route of 8 to 11.5 miles. Number of stiles; Shorter Route:- 33, Longer Route:- 45.

General Notes: The Forhill Picnic Place is ideal to visit the countryside south of Birmingham. The walk uses small sections of the **NWP**, (see Page 7), and also The Icknield Way, (Two walks by the North Worcestershire Countryside Action Project, (NWCAP). The Longer Route uses paths on the county boundary with Birmingham.

Route Notes: From the Picnic Place cross the grass by the toilets, **(NWP** sign), then cross a road into Lea End Lane, passing 'The Peacock' on the left. (Too early for a drink?). Follow the lane for 300 yards, cross a stile on the left, and follow the path through the wood. Cross a ditch-crossing, (DC), and stile, then turn right.

Cross another stile, walk parallel to the hedge on the right and in the next field follow the right fence, (ahead/right are the Lickey Hills, **Walk 7**). Cross an open field to a stile by a gate, (farm buildings visible further back), then go part left, following the left tree line. At the bottom corner of the field cross stile and DC to a road, go left for 20 yards, then turn right into Stonehouse Lane.

150 yards along the lane cross a stile on the right, follow the right hedge/fence, (the farm on the right is the one in view earlier), and reach the far right corner of the field. Cross two stiles with a DC between, (CAREFUL - DEEP DITCH), and again go to the far right corner. Once over the stile keep generally to the right side of the field, (possibly overgrown), and after 75 yards cross a stile on the right. Now follow the left fence as it curves left, then cross a stile and DC to rejoin Lea End Lane.

Here turn left and follow the lane for about 400 yards, then cross a DC and stile on the left, (opposite some cottages, one with an unusual gateway, see Page 46). Once over go part right and cross the open field, (no clear aiming point, just keep to the centre of the field), until a stile is visible in the far fence.

45

Cross this, (or around if fence removed), and go 45° right, aiming for a gap in the trees. Cross a stile, (hidden until reached), at the right end of the gap, then follow the right fence before crossing the end of a field to a stile by a gate. Cross the road and in the next field aim for the large isolated tree to the left of the electric poles. Continue directly ahead up the open field to a stile in a fence. Now go part left to a stile by the end of the trees to the left. (Not easily visible until reached).

Cross the road and then go part right, up a large open field, aiming for a large tree to the left of an electricity pole. (At 100 yards across the field the route passes over the 2726 yards long Wast Hill tunnel of the Worcester and Birmingham Canal, an indirect link with **Walks 1 & 8**). Cross a stile, follow the right hedge for 100 yards and cross a stile on the right. Now go 45° left to a stile to the road and turn left.

Follow the road for 200 yards, around a bend, then cross a stile on the right, rejoining the **NWP**. Follow the right hedge, over further stiles, (and again over the Wast Hill tunnel), to enter a wood and soon join an old tarmac drive. Shortly after leaving the trees, (view left towards Birmingham and right into Worcestershire), take a path on the right, (the **NWP**), where the tarmac drive sweeps left. Follow the path over a stile and after 20 yards reach a stile on the left. This is **Point A**, the turn off for the Longer Route. Having made a choice see Page 47.

Unusual **Garden Gate** *on the first part of* **Walk 9**.

Shorter Route, from Point A: **Do not** cross the stile on the left but continue on the **NWP**, hedge on left, crossing two stiles. Ignore gates on the left then, with farm buildings visible ahead, cross a stile on the left and turn right. Follow the right fence/hedge passing raised ground, (an old pond). Continue towards the far right corner of the field, (still **NWP**), to a stile on the right, this is **Point B** on the map. Now see the bottom of this page and the heading, **"Route Back from Point B"**.

Longer Route, from Point A: Cross the stile on the left and follow it through the wood, fence on the right, to reach a road. (This path is a Right of Way, the tarmac drive to the left is not). Cross the road and through the gate of Redhill Farm, immediately go left and once in the field turn right. Follow the field edge past the farm buildings, (on the right), and go through a gate into the next field. Immediately go through the gate on the right, turn left and follow the left hedge.

Now go through the right gate of the two gates ahead and follow the left fence, (the boundary between Birmingham and Worcestershire, the OS map incorrectly shows the path in Birmingham). Follow the left hedge as it 'dog-legs' to reach a gap in the hedge ahead. In the next field go 45° right to reach a lane via a gate or stile and turn left. Follow the lane for 100 yards and, where it bends right, keep straight ahead on a wide track, (a bridlepath, muddy in places), for 600 yards to reach a road and turn right. (A footpath in the field on the right is not used and is usually overgrown).

Proceed along the road to 100 yards beyond a cross-roads and turn right over a DC, (NB, DEEP ditch), and two stiles to a field. Go across the open field to a stile between some trees then aim for the right end of the buildings ahead. Negotiate a series of stiles and gates, cross a lane and then a DC and stile opposite.

Cross the open field, initially following some dead trees, to a stile some 20 yards left of the far right corner. Go through an overgrown site to a stile in the far wire fence, then left to a stile to a lane, but **do not** cross. Turn around (back to the stile), and cross the field, (the **correct** Right of Way), towards the centre of the opposite hedge.

Cross a stile by a gate, continue over the next field to a stile at the right end of the tree line. Now go generally left to meet the left hedge, follow this, hedge on the left, then over the field corner to a stile and DC to a lane. Turn left, cross a busy road, go over the stile into a large field, then follow a row of trees on the left, (old hedge line). At the **far end** of the field, at the last of a row of six trees, turn left, joining the **NWP**, and proceed to a stile near the far right corner. This is **Point B** on the map.

Route Back from Point B: Cross the stile, (and DC), turn left and follow the track to 'The Peacock'. For those that can resist the temptation of the hostelry turn left, then cross a road and go over the stile and back to the start start (P.K. 8/97).

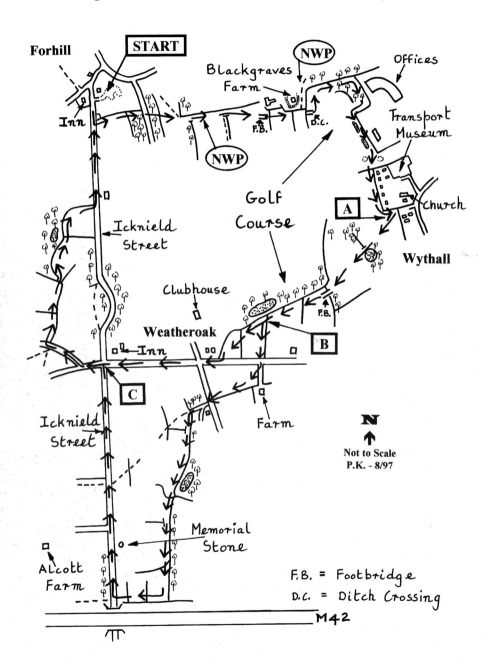

Forhill

START

Blackgraves Farm

NWP

Offices

Inn

F.B.

NWP

D.C.

Transport Museum

Golf Course

A

Church

Wythall

Icknield Street

Clubhouse

Weatheroak

Inn

F.B.

B

C

Icknield Street

Farm

N

Not to Scale
P.K. - 8/97

Memorial Stone

Alcott Farm

F.B. = Footbridge
D.C. = Ditch Crossing

M42

The **River Severn, Diglis Lock** *and* **Worcester Cathedral,** *(on Walk 1).*

The Staffordshire and Worcestershire Canal, near Cookley, (on Walk 4)

Eckington Bridge *from* **Eckington Wharf Picnic Place,** *(at the start of Walk 16).*

The prominent landmark of Tardebigge Church spire, (by the start of Walk 8)

WALK 10   FORHILL and WYTHALL   4 or 5.5 Miles

Start: The County Council Picnic Place at Forhill. (GR. 055755).

Parking: At the Worcestershire County Council Picnic Place, as above.

Refreshments: 'The Peacock', (at start), or the 'Coach and Horses', (on route).

O.S. Maps: Pathfinder 954 (Solihull), and Landranger 139 (Birmingham).

Summary: A walk to Wythall utilising parts of the **North Worcestershire Path**, **(NWP)**, 'The Icknield Way', (two County Council circular routes), and also the old Roman road. This walk can also be linked with **Walk 9** to give a route length of 8 to 11.5 miles. (**NB**, the **Route Map** for this walk is on **Page 48**, prior to the colour inserts). Number of stiles; Shorter Route:- 21, Longer Route:- 27.

General Notes: The original intention was a route across fields and around Alcott Farm but the construction of a motorway noise reduction barrier, just south of the farm, has resulted in the current format. **Walks 9** and **10** have been designed to link together to give longer walk options for the more energetic rambler.

Route Notes: From the Picnic Place entrance turn left and walk along Icknield Street, (Ryknild St. on OS map), for about 200 yards and turn left over a stile. The initial part of the route is on the **North Worcestershire Path**, **(NWP)**. Follow the left field edge, cross a stile into the trees, then cross more stiles and a road to enter a field. Go part right, (no definite aiming point though the path should be evident), and cross the open field towards the trees in the opposite hedge.

At the tree line go through a wide gap in the fence/hedge and follow the left hedge. (The large building in the distance ahead is the Britannic Assurance Company office, passed later on the route). On nearing farm buildings (Blackgraves Farm, a 17th century moated farmhouse), head for the right end of the farm buildings. Negotiate some piles of rubble, cross a footbridge and stile, then go part left to another stile.

Follow the left fence, (moat and farmhouse on left), ignore the stile on the left and cross the stile, (and **narrow ditch-crossing**), ahead, leaving the **NWP**. At the Kings Norton Golf Course turn left and follow the left edge of the Course as it sweeps around to the right. (Watch out for flying golf balls!). Follow the well-marked path, (yellow waymarks and yellow topped posts), as it meanders through trees and open areas to eventually join the fence of the Britannic Assurance Co. complex. The compound, (left, beyond the fence), was the site of RAF Wythall, a Balloon Barrage Centre. It was later a car depot and is now an office complex.

49

Continue to follow the left fence, Golf Course over to the right, and eventually emerge onto the Course between two 'Tee' positions. Go between these to the fence opposite, (mobile homes beyond), and turn right. After 20 yards turn left, over a stile and narrow DC, to follow the left fence as it turns left to reach a left hand corner with wooden sheds ahead. This is **Point A** on the map. If visiting Wythall Church and the Transport Museum see below, if not see "**Route from Point A**" below.

Route to Wythall Church: Continue ahead past the wood sheds, (on the right), turn left at the road and reach the church. St Mary's Church was built in 1862 but is now derelict, although many of the graves are still attended to. The Transport Museum is located down Severn Way and the caravan site has a small shop. To continue the walk return to **Point A.**

Route from Point A: From the corner of the field, (with your back to the same), go diagonally across the open field towards the left side of a gap in the middle distance tree line, (please see the map). Go through a small gap in the hedge close to the left tree line, (the deep pit is an old pond). Now go slightly left across another open field, generally aiming mid way between the two buildings visible on the horizon ahead, (a house to the left/and the golf Clubhouse to the right).

When about halfway across the field a yellow topped marker post should be visible, located about 100 yards from the far left corner of the field. Pass the marker, cross a footbridge then follow the right fence, the Golf Course on the other side. Continue over one stile and on to the stile in the far right corner of the next field, (pond on the right), and cross, this is **Point B** and decision time; 4 miles or 5.5 miles.

Shorter Route, Pt. B to Pt. C: Having crossed the stile go only part left and up the field to a stile by a gate. Cross and proceed to the top left field corner to a stile to the road. Now turn right and follow the road, (choose the side where you are most visible to traffic from both directions), and reach a cross-roads and the 'Coach and Horses' inn, Point C on the map. Now see the next page, **"Return from Point C"**.

Longer Route, Pt. B to Pt. C: Once over the stile turn left and proceed to a stile by an oak tree about 30 yards from the top left field corner. Cross the road, go 40 yards up the farm drive and cross a stile on the right. Now go part left to reach the left fence/hedge and follow it, fence on the left, to a stile to another road.

Cross the road, go along a house drive and, as it bends left, keep ahead on a track. Cross a stile by a gate and turn left, following the left hedge, with views ahead across Worcestershire to the Cotswolds and Bredon Hill, (**Walk 14**). Cross a stile at the bottom left corner of the field and then over a further stile to reach the fence of the M42. Here turn right and, via two stiles or gates, reach Icknield St and turn right.

Follow the lane passing, on the right, a stone marked 'JD 1885', this marks the spot where a policeman, P.C. James Davies, was murdered in 1885. Pass two stiles on either side of the road, the original intended route but not used due to motorway work by Alcott Farm, and continue to the 'Coach and Horses', **Point C** on the map.

Return from Point C: With your back to the inn entrance turn right and follow the main road, going past Icknield Street, for 200 yards. (There is a shorter route back by following Icknield Street, but that's cheating). Turn right along a country lane for 400 yards and cross a stile on the right. Now generally follow the right hedge, cross another stile and go up to a stile tucked into the top right corner of the field. Cross this, go up some steps, and now follow the left hedge.

Whilst there should be no need to rest whilst going up Swan's Hill, it is worthwhile turning around to admire the view, (left to right), of the Cotswolds, the tip of the Malvern Hills and then, on the right, the Lickey Hills. Having admired the view turn around and continue as before, following the left hedge and over more stiles to reach Icknield Street. Here turn left and follow Icknield Street back to the Forhill Picnic Place, (and 'The Peacock' to celebrate a safe return!).   (P.K. 8/97).

'The Peacock' *at* **Forhill**, *(Walks 9 and 10)*.

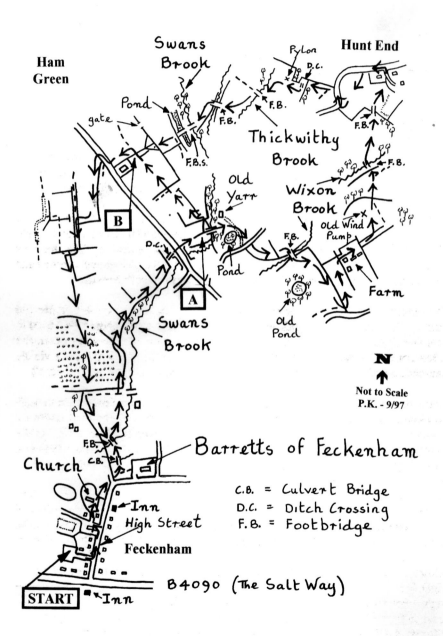

Swans Brook

Ham Green

Hunt End

Pylon

D.C.

Pond

gate

F.B.

F.B.

Thickwithy Brook

F.B.

F.B.S.

Old Yarr

Wixon Brook

F.B.

Old Wind Pump

B

D.C.

F.B.

A

Pond

Farm

Swans Brook

Old Pond

N

Not to Scale
P.K. - 9/97

Church

C.B.

F.B.

Barretts of Feckenham

Inn

High Street

Feckenham

C.B. = Culvert Bridge
D.C. = Ditch Crossing
F.B. = Footbridge

B4090 (The Salt Way)

START

Inn

52

WALK 11   **FECKENHAM, HUNT END and**   **3 or 5 Miles**
                           HAM GREEN

Start: The village of Feckenham. (GR. 008614).

Parking: The public car park off High Street. (Signposted).

Refreshments: Two inns in Feckenham, none on the route.

O.S. Maps: Pathfinder 975 (Redditch) and Landranger 150 (Worcester).

Summary: A walk north of Feckenham, through fields and over brooks, towards Hunt End and Ham Green. It links with Walk 12 to create a route of 7.5 miles to 13 miles. Number of stiles; Shorter Route:- 21, Longer Route:- 41.

General Notes: Feckenham village was once at the centre of the Royal Forest of Feckenham, remnants of which survive at Chaddesley Wood by Chaddesley Corbett. The trees were felled to provide fuel for salt making at Droitwich. The area now attracts many walkers and outdoor enthusiasts, both for the pleasant countryside and to visit 'Barretts of Feckenham'. This walk can combine both activities.

Route Notes: From the car park return to High Street and turn left. After 100 yards, at The Square, go slightly left and follow the path to the church, dedicated to St. John The Baptist. The church has Norman origins with a 15th century tower, and i⁄has not escaped the attention of the Victorians. (The benefit of this route via the church is avoiding the temptation of passing the 'Rose & Crown' public house!).

Leave the churchyard at the north-east corner via a gate and a pathway, then through two kissing gates either side of a drive. Here, with Barretts of Feckenham directly ahead, the route is left, following the left hedge. (However, a detour to view future purchases might be in order). Follow the left hedge over a culvert bridge, (stiles), a footbridge, (FB), over Swans Brook, and then sweep around to the right.

Cross the end of the field, brook to the right, then go over a stile into a field. The route now **generally** follows the line of the brook, (on the right), over four stiles and a ditch crossing to reach a road. Cross this, go through an iron gate and over a field, brook to the right, to a FB over Swans Brook. This is **Point A** and a choice of route.

Shorter Route, Pt. A to Pt. B: **Do not** cross the FB but turn left and follow the right fence. Cross a stile in the corner, go left through a hedge gap and then turn right. Follow the right hedge, cross a stile ahead, then go over the field to an iron gate on the far side. Go through and turn left. This is **Point B**, now see Page 55 and **"Route Back from Point B"**. (This shorter route cuts out 20 stiles and 8 FBs, pity!).

Longer Route, Pt. A to Pt. B: Cross the footbridge into the beautifully kept grounds of 'Old Yarr', (please respect the privacy of the owners). Skirt the left edge of the pond, then cross the drive to reach a stile 30 yards to the left of the drive entrance. Cross a lane, go through the metal gate opposite and turn part left, generally following the Wixon Brook to the right.

Go through another iron gate, follow the brook for 50 yards then cross it via a FB. Once over go part left to join a fence and turn right, following the fence to the top left corner. Cross the stile on the left, then go part left and diagonally across the field to the left end of the farm buildings. Go through a metal gate and across the centre of a field, farm buildings to the right, to reach two gates in the far fence.

Go through the gate to the right, follow the track for about 100 yards, then go under the single strand barbed wire fence on the left. Once under go part right, passing an old wind pump, to the bottom of the field, (see map), and cross a stile. (The route here joins '**The Monarch's Way**' for a short time, see Page 7). Now go straight across the flat section of the field heading towards a gap in the trees ahead.

By a large gate cross a stile and a bridge over the Wixon Brook, go part right and across the open field to a FB in the hedge line ahead. Once over again go part right and walk towards the house. (The land to the right is the remains of an old moated enclosure). Cross a stile, go through a small gate and turn left up the drive. At the road turn left for 75 yards and cross a stile on the left. Now go part right and across the same field as before to a stile by a gate. (N.B. the tempting short cut across the bottom of the field is not a Right of Way, the route as described is).

Cross the stile to a lane, turn right and after 50 yards cross a stile on the left. Now follow the fence on the right, (ignore a track going left), to cross another stile. Once over turn left and over a ditch crossing, turn right and then cross an open field, keeping just left of an electricity pylon. At the far hedge turn left and follow the right hedge to reach a FB over the Thickwithey Brook, just past some trees. Cross this and turn left, (ignoring the stile visible on the opposite side of field). Follow the left hedge for about 100 yards and then go part right, crossing the field to yet another FB. Once over again turn left.

Follow the left hedge and cross two FBs at the far corner, (the first over Swans Brook and the next over an elongated pond). Cross a wire fence with old tree stumps for a cross-step, (could be painful for men with short legs), then go straight across an open field towards a group of trees. Cross a stile then follow the right hedge for about 200 yards, (negotiating a wire fence that should now have a stile installed), to a large metal gate on the right. Go though and turn left, this is **Point B** on the map. Now see Page 55 and **"Route Back from Point B"**.

Route Back from Point B: Follow the left fence/hedge to a stile and steps down to a lane. Go right for 40 yards, pass a gate, then cross a stile on the left. Now follow the left hedge to the very far left corner of the field, turn right and down the field to another stile. Once over turn left and follow a wide track. (This track was part of an old road shown on maps in the mid 19th century).

On reaching an open field turn right and follow the right hedge to the corner, here cross a stile and turn left. Follow the left hedge and, as this goes sharp left, continue ahead across the open field to a stile in the hedge. (Aim to the right of the electricity pylon visible ahead). Once over the stile aim for the large tree ahead, then follow the line of trees as they curve gently to the right.

Cross the stile ahead, (by the metal gate), keeping the same direction and now following the fence on the right. (Ignore the gates in it as these go to the farm over to the right). Reach and return over the footbridge across Swans Brook and retrace the route back to the car park. (Alternatively, the opportunity can be taken to visit Barretts of Feckenham and return via the High Street and, this time, call at the 'Rose and Crown'!).   (P.K. 9/97).

The pond at **Morton Underhill**, *the* 'crossover place', **(Point C)**, *on Walk 12.*

55

Map for Walk 12   Feckenham and Inkberrow Circular

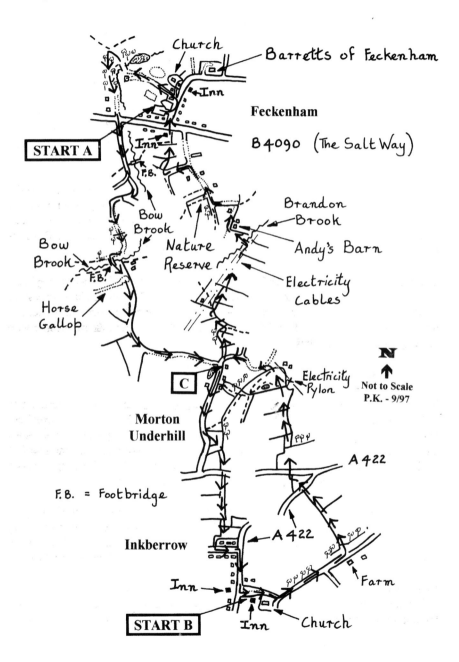

Church

Barretts of Feckenham

Inn

Feckenham

B4090 (The Salt Way)

START A

Inn

F.B.

Bow Brook

Brandon Brook

Nature Reserve

Andy's Barn

Bow Brook

Electricity Cables

F.B.

Horse Gallop

N

↑
Not to Scale
P.K. - 9/97

C

Electricity Pylon

Morton Underhill

A 422

F.B. = Footbridge

A 422

Inkberrow

Inn →

Farm

START B   Inn   Church

WALK 12   FECKENHAM and INKBERROW Circular   3.5 to 8 Miles

Start: ˙   From Feckenham, the car park off High Street, (GR. 008614),
or from Inkberrow, by 'The Old Bull', (GR. 016573).

Parking: The public car park off High Street at Feckenham; limited
street parking in Inkberrow, (but see **General Notes** below).

Refreshments: Inns at both Feckenham and Inkberrow, no others on the route.

O.S. Maps: Pathfinder 975 (Redditch) and 997 (Stratford upon Avon). Also
Landranger 150 (Worcester).

Summary: A walk linking Feckenham, **(START A)**, and Inkberrow, **(START
B)**, in a double loop joined at Morton Underhill, **(Point C)**; giving a 4.5 mile route
from Feckenham, a 3.5 mile route from Inkberrow, or a full route of 8 miles. It can
be linked with **Walk 11** to give a route of 7.5 miles to 13 miles. Maximum No. of
stiles:- 14. ('Barretts of Feckenham' is just north of **START A**).

General Notes: The area between the two villages has many 'Rights of Way' and
this route uses only a few of them. It mainly keeps to bridlepaths as they are easy to
follow and also minimises the number of stiles. Parking at Inkberrow is somewhat
limited but the owner of 'The Old Bull', at the 'Village Green', allows people who
patronise the inn to use their car park when doing walks.

Route Notes:

START A to Point C: From the car park return to High Street and turn left. After
100 yards again turn left into The Square and continue into Mill Lane. (Feckenham
church is to the right, see notes in **Walk 11**). Follow Mill Lane, which soon becomes
a gravel track, past cottages and the Cricket Club. At a path junction near The Old
Mill House keep right, passing the house, (left), and the mill pond (right). Cross a
footbridge and continue up a wide bridlepath to a path cross-roads.

Now turn left, signposted Salt Way and Morton Underhill, and follow the bridlepath
to the B4090, (the Salt Way, a Roman road to Droitwich). Cross the road, going
slightly right, and go along a narrow tarmac lane, the Bow Brook on the left. As the
lane turns right keep straight ahead, via a metal gate and then follow the right hedge.

Keep following the right hedge as it sweeps to the right, go through another metal
gate and continue following the hedge to the far right corner of the field. Now turn
left and follow an enclosed track, a quite discernible old track featured on old maps.

Continue along the well-defined bridlepath then, 200 yards beyond a metal bridlegate, turn right, Bow Brook again to the left. Some 100 yards after the turn go left, over a footbridge, then continue ahead, with a hedge left and an open field right. Cross over a 'horse gallop' and continue following the left hedge, passing through several fields, (and no stiles, all on a bridlepath). Eventually the route sweeps left, through a large gap in the hedge, and follows a wide track that leads to the hamlet of Morton Underhill, this is **Point C** on the map, the route intersection.

Point C to START B: With the pond on the right, (house left), follow the tarmac lane south past farm buildings. Some 600 yards beyond the pond cross a stile on the left, (the second of two stiles), and go part right, across and up the field, to a stile near the opposite corner. (The view right includes the Malvern, Abberley and Clee Hills). Go over the stile, follow the right hedge to a lane and cross it.

Go through a gate and follow the left hedge, the Cotswold Ridge ahead/left and Bredon Hill ahead/right. Go through a hedge gap, (or a stile if the fence replaced), and proceed to the far left corner of the second field. Cross a stile and follow the right hedge. Cross another stile and follow the right side of the playing fields and, in the far right corner, follow a path that goes right and left to a lane. Now turn left, go to the A422, turn right, and follow it to Inkberrow 'Village Green' and the two inns.

START B to Point C: From the 'Village Green', with your back to The Old Bull, (well; you have to leave sometime!), turn right and walk down the lane past the church. (St. Peter's Church is mainly of 15th century construction and has a prominent setting when viewed from the east). At a 'T' junction turn left and follow the old, part sunken lane, passing a road junction to reach a farm, (on the right).

Some 30 yards past the farmhouse turn left, then use the gate to the right and keep the same direction, hedge on the left. Proceed via a stile and gate to the A422, cross this and the stile opposite. Go to the far left corner of the field, through a gate in the left fence, then over a stile on the right Cross the lane and go through a bridlegate.

Follow the wide track across the field towards the trees, go through two gates close together, and follow the right hedge. Go through two more fields and reach a bridlegate near to an electric pylon. (A direct route from here to Morton Underhill, going down the steep hill to a gate at the bottom left corner, could be difficult in wet conditions so it has not been used. The paths are, however, shown on the map).

Now go part left and diagonally across the field, passing old cars and farm implements, to a metal gate at the far side. Go through, immediately turn sharp left, and follow an old, wooded track, (possibly muddy), downhill. At the bottom join a tarmac lane that turns left to reach Morton Underhill, **Point C** on the map.

Point C to START A: With the pond left, and a house right, follow the tarmac lane north. Just before it turns right keep ahead into a field and follow the left hedge. Cross a stile and continue following the left hedge as it sweeps right. Go over a stile, then through a gate on the left, and now turn right.

Follow the right hedge, go through another metal gate, (electricity poles to the left), and continue to the far right corner of the field. Go through the gate on the right, (keeping to the bridlepath), and follow the left hedge and go through another gate. Continue following a left hedge, go through a bridlegate and across an open field, passing under the first line of electric cables, to reach a gate near the far left corner.

Once through follow the track to the next gate and cross the bridge over the Brandon Brook. Follow the track as it turns to the left, (fence on the right), and reach, via another gate, a large barn. At the end of the barn turn right and follow a stony track past more buildings, (Andy's Barn), heading towards a house. Go past the house, (another gate), turn left and follow the drive to a 'T' junction, here turn right.

Follow this wide track, (the Wylde Moor Nature Reserve on the left), going gently uphill. Just prior to some terraced houses on the right, turn left onto a wide track. Follow this, via another gate, to reach an open field ahead. Now turn right, cross a stile, then two fields and two more stiles, to reach the car park of 'The Lygon Arms'. Ramblers not visiting this establishment should follow the footpath to the right of the car park, cross the B4090 into High Street and then to **'START A'.**

(P.K. 9/97).

The Old Bull *at* **Inkberrow**, *(START B of Walk 12).*

Map for Walk 13   Fish Hill, Broadway Tower and Broadway

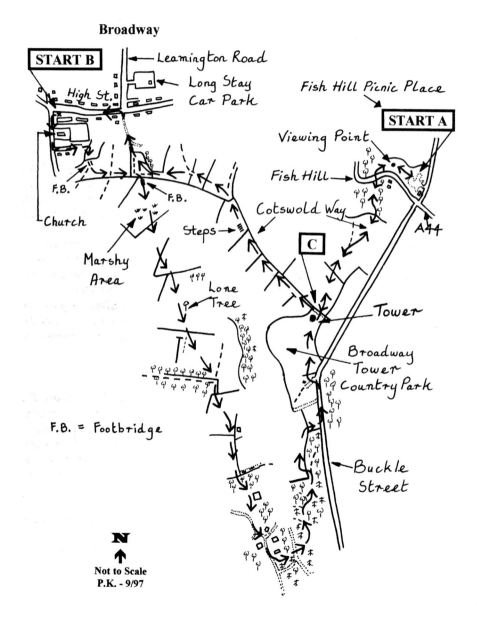

Broadway

START B

Leamington Road

Long Stay
Car Park

High St.

Fish Hill Picnic Place

START A

Viewing Point

Fish Hill

F.B.

F.B.

Cotswold Way

Church

Steps

C

A44

Marshy
Area

Lone
Tree

Tower

Broadway
Tower
Country Park

F.B. = Footbridge

Buckle
Street

N
↑
Not to Scale
P.K. - 9/97

FISH HILL, BROADWAY TOWER   4 or 5.5 Miles
                        and BROADWAY

Start: From the Fish Hill Picnic Place, (**START A**, GR. 121369), or
                   from Broadway, (**START B**, GR. 095375).

Parking: At the Fish Hill Picnic Place, (free), or Broadway, (chargeable).

Refreshments: Numerous places in Broadway or, (for fee paying visitors), the
                   cafe at the Broadway Tower Country Park.

O.S. Maps: Pathfinder 1043 (Broadway) or Landranger 150 (Worcester).

Summary: A walk linking the Fish Hill Picnic Place, Broadway and the
Broadway Tower Country Park, using a section of the **Cotswold Way**, (see Page 7),
and some lesser used paths. Choose a clear day for the views across Worcestershire
to Wales and Shropshire. Number of stiles; Shorter Route:- 12, Longer Route:- 14.

General Notes: The top of Broadway, (or Beacon), Hill offers superb views across
Worcestershire and is accessible by car, (but that's cheating). The choice of starting
points allows the uphill section to be at the beginning or end of the walk, but the
Shorter Route can only be done by starting from Broadway, (**START B**). The
Broadway Tower Country Park is privately owned and, whilst walkers may use the
Rights of Way free of charge, a fee is payable if visiting the cafe, the tower or the
Park. Footpaths north of the A44 could not be used because of bypass construction.

Route Notes:

Fish Hill to Broadway, (from START A): From the Picnic Place follow the
signs to the 'Viewing Point', to look towards, (trees permitting), Worcestershire,
Warwickshire and Gloucestershire. Having admired the 'view' continue ahead, on
a permissive path, and after 40 yards keep left, following the **Cotswold Way** signs.
VERY CAREFULLY cross the A44 and follow the meandering path through woods,
(yellow waymarks). Cross a stile, go over fields towards the tower, and to the fence
of the Broadway Tower Country Park, (see **General Notes**), **Point C** on the map.

Do not enter the country park but turn right, (**NB**, ramblers leaving the Country Park
on the Shorter Route **turn left**), still following the **Cotswold Way**, (only 8 stiles to
START B!). Enjoy the downhill walk with continuous views over Worcestershire
to Wales and Shropshire. The route follows the fence/wall on the right, goes down
some steps then, after another stile, crosses an open section of field.

After passing through an old gateway, (no gate), leave the **Cotswold Way**, (which veers to the right), by keeping ahead and then towards the left hedge. Pass through a short, enclosed, section of path, cross a stile, then go part right towards the end of a line of trees. Continue past the end of the trees, (same direction), to reach the far corner of the field. Cross the stile, follow a track to a tarmac drive, and then follow this to the High Street. Here turn left and proceed past shops and 'fleshpots' to the War Memorial at the bottom of the High Street, (**START B**).

Broadway to Fish Hill (from START B):   From the War Memorial at the bottom of High Street go past the Broadway Hotel and turn left into Church Street. Go past the 'Crown and Trumpet'(!) and to the Parish Church, (St. Michael and All Angels, built in the 19th century). Once past the church turn left into a cobbled street and then onto a concrete drive. Go through a kissing gate (KG) and keep ahead, through trees, to a KG to a field, (Broadway Tower visible directly ahead). Here **turn right**, follow the right tree line, cross a stile and a footbridge and turn left.

Again follow the right tree line, the Cotswold Escarpment now directly ahead. **Pass** a stile on the right and reach the far right corner of the field. Cross a stile, continue ahead for some 50 yards, then cross a stile and footbridge on the right. Now for the interesting part of the walk, the route is now diagonally across five fields with the path not always apparent. However, have faith and trust the good guidebook!.

From the footbridge go part left across the open field and gently uphill, (look for a stile in the hedge ahead). Go over, or around, a marshy area, (care needed), cross the stile and continue in the same direction. As the next hedge comes into view aim for a stile to the right of a tree. Now cross the corner of a field to the next stile.

Continue in the same general direction, over another field, keeping to the right of a lone tree, to reach a stile by a metal gate. Now for a good test of navigational skills!. Maintain the same direction going diagonally, (left), across the open field, (do not be misled by the horse track going straight ahead). Continue across the field to eventually reach a stile and gate by a hedge corner, (if in doubt refer to the map).

Cross the stile and follow an enclosed track, (ignore the downhill track right), to another stile and gate. Now go part left, over a field, towards a house, (to the right are Bredon Hill and the Malvern Hills). Pass the house, (on the left), cross a stile and follow the left fence. At a path junction keep ahead, via a gate, into woodland.

Follow the track through the wood, pass a house on the left, then join a tarmac drive. Follow the drive as it passes some ornate dwellings and becomes a gravel track. Some 100 yards past the last building on the left look for a narrow path sweeping left into the trees. (This path is easy to miss so please watch carefully).

Follow this path as it becomes a wide track going directly uphill. Pass a fence on the right, (watch out for the Pheasant Plucker!), cross another track and continue uphill. Soon the path sweeps gently left and right and levels out. Now watch for a gate and stile, some 15 yards to the left, leaving the more prominent path through the wood.

Having crossed the stile turn right and follow the right fence/wall, (taking time to admire the view to the left). Follow the wall as it sweeps right, cross a stile into the Broadway Tower Country Park, (see **General Notes**), and continue to a road. (This is Buckle Street, the boundary between Worcestershire and Gloucestershire).

Turn left, follow the road for 200 yards and cross a stile on the left, re-entering the Country Park. Go part right, through a large KG, passing to the right of Broadway Tower, (a folly, built in the late 18th century for the Earl of Coventry). Exit the park at another large KG, (**Point C** on the map). (Ramblers not going to the Fish Hill Picnic Place should **turn left** here to go back to Broadway, see Page 61).

To reach START A, (Fish Hill Picnic Place), maintain the same direction as before, joining the **Cotswold Way** and crossing open land. Go through a gate, then past old quarry workings, (now grassed), to reach a stile to a wood. Follow the meandering path through the wood, (watch for the yellow waymarks), and reach the A44. VERY CAREFULLY cross the road, then take the path sweeping right to the 'Viewing Point' and then to the main car park of the Fish Hill Picnic Place.   P.K. 9/97.

Broadway Tower *at the* **Broadway Tower Country Park**, *(Walk 13)*.

Map for Walk 14   Elmley Castle, Bredon Hill & Gt. Comberton

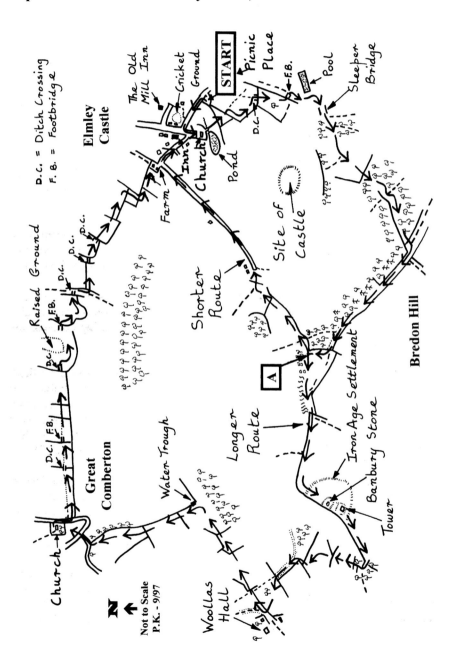

D.C. = Ditch Crossing
F.B. = Footbridge

Elmley Castle

The Old Mill Inn

Cricket Ground

START

Picnic Place

F.B.

Pool

Sleeper Bridge

Inn

Church

Pond

D.C.

Site of Castle

Raised Ground

D.C.

D.C.

F.B.

D.C.

Farm

Shorter Route

Bredon Hill

A

Iron Age Settlement

Banbury Stone

D.C. F.B.

Great Comberton

Water Trough

Longer Route

Tower

Church

N

Not to Scale
P.K. - 9/97

Woollas Hall

ELMLEY CASTLE, BREDON HILL   **3.5 or 7.5 Miles**
                    and GREAT COMBERTON

Start: Elmley Castle Picnic Place, (GR. 985411).

Parking: At the Picnic Place, signposted from the main street.

Refreshments: Two inns in the village, (please see the map, The Old Mill Inn
                    has good food and interesting wines). No places on the route.

O.S. Maps: Explorer 14 (Malvern Hills) and Landranger 150 (Worcester).

Summary: A walk over Bredon Hill, on part of the **Wychavon Way**, to enjoy
the view over Worcestershire. The Longer Route goes via the tower and visits Great
Comberton. Number of stiles; Shorter Route:- 3, Longer Route:- 27.

General Notes: This is an area steeped in history, from the Iron Age settlement on
Bredon Hill to the visit of Queen Elizabeth I to Elmley Castle. It is a walk that
should be done on a clear day, to enjoy the views across the Worcestershire Plain.

Route Notes: From the Picnic Place go to the road, then left into the village, then
left again to the church, (Saint Mary the Virgin). The church has Norman origins
and is very interesting. Exit the churchyard beyond the tower, passing a pond on the
right. Cross a stile to a field and continue ahead to another stile.

Enter a large open field and turn right, following the right hedge around the field.
(Here the Right of Way is via the centre of the field but, as it is difficult to follow or
mark, the permissive path around the field edge is normally used). Some 50 yards
before the far right corner cross a ditch crossing, (DC), and stile on the right. Now
go slightly left, (and left of a large oak tree), to a stile in the left fence. Cross this,
and a footbridge, (FB), then turn right onto the **Wychavon Way**. (See Page 7).

The route now follows the **Wychavon Way**, (**W** symbol), to the plateau of Bredon
Hill. Continue uphill, through a bridlegate, pass an elongated pool on the left, then
swing right over a wide 'railway sleeper' bridge. There are a number of tracks here
so watch for the **W** symbol, the path becoming more obvious as it passes through
trees. (The high ground over to the right is the site of the castle, now demolished).

Continue up the hill on an indistinct path, (follow the **W** symbol), ignoring a path
going to the castle site, (Broadway Tower, **Walk 13**, visible to the left). Go through
a bridlegate, enter woodland, and at a wire fence turn left and right to follow it to the
summit plateau. Go through a gate and turn right, leaving the **Wychavon Way**.

Follow the wide bridlepath with trees to the right. (Here do not look left to avoid the temptation of Gloucestershire, beyond Bredon Hill!). Keep on this track which becomes narrower, ignore a bridlegate on the right going into the wood, and soon reach a large gate to a field. Once through turn right and, at the bottom right corner, reach a path junction. This is **Point A** on the map and a choice of route.

Shorter Route from Point A: At the path junction turn right and follow the wide track that sweeps gently right and downhill. Ignore a bridlegate, (right), and a track, (left), and meander downhill, with views over the Vale of Evesham. Go through a gate then, at a path junction, turn right. Now follow the wide stony track, via a bridlegate and a sunken track, to a tarmac lane leading back to Elmley Castle.

Longer Route from Point A: At the path junction turn left, going back uphill, keeping to the right side of the field. Again reach the summit plateau with views north, weather permitting, over the Worcestershire Plain, to the Malvern, Abberley, Clent, Waseley and Lickey Hills, all at the County boundary. A place to linger.

Having sampled the views proceed westward, through a gate, following the wall on the right to reach the ancient hill settlement, the Banbury Stone, and the stone tower. (The tower, known as Parson's Folly, now festooned with radio aerials, was built in the late 18th century. The Banbury Stone is also known as the Elephant Stone because of its shape). The route continues along the wall, past the tower, and sweeps right into the trees. Once past the trees **turn right** onto a path that goes downhill.

Cross a metal gate with a stile and follow a wide grassy track downhill. Cross a stile in a fence, bearing slightly left over an open field, towards the left end of the wood ahead. Some 100 yards before reaching the trees turn left, going downhill to a stile, by a gate, in the bottom right corner. Cross and go to a 'T' junction, turn left, then follow the farm track downhill. (The village ahead is Birlingham, **Walk 16**).

Cross the stile near the metal gate and go part left, away from the farm track, aiming to the right of the building below, (Woollas Hall). Cross the stile in front of the drive and turn right, (do not follow the drive), and continue along the right fence. Go through a metal gate, initially follow a fence on the left and then go over an open field. Keep the same direction, crossing two more stiles, then over another open field to reach a fence corner by a water trough.

Here turn left, (through an old fence line), and follow the right fence/hedge, crossing two stiles. Now go part right to follow a ditch on the right. At the bottom right corner of the field cross a stile to the road, turn right, and go into Great Comberton. At a road junction continue ahead, on a footpath, to reach the village church, St Michael's, which also has Norman origins.

Leave the churchyard by the gate on the east side, turn right and follow the lane for 150 yards. Now go left, over a stile, on a footpath signposted to Elmley Castle. Follow the generally enclosed path, (keep to the right hedge), over stiles, a DC and FB, to reach a stile and DC with rising ground ahead. Here turn right for about 40 yards and then turn left to follow the right hedge.

At the next hedgeline ahead turn left then, after 30 yards, cross a FB and stile on the right. Once through the brambles go to the right, following the right tree line around the curving edge of the field. Cross a stile and DC to a track, turn right, then after 40 yards turn left, over a stile, into a field. Now follow the left fence/hedge to the left field corner, cross two stiles with a DC between, and then follow the hedge/fence on the right.

Cross yet another DC and stile and go over the field to the far right corner. Cross a stile, follow the right hedge/fence to the next corner, then go right, through a gate or gap. Go along the left hedge, cross a stile, turn left and again follow the left hedge, going through fields and crossing two more stiles. Go through farm gates, passing barns on the right, to the far left corner behind the second barn. Here turn right, cross a stile, and follow an enclosed path to the farm entrance. Now turn left into a lane and follow it back to the main street of Elmley Castle. From there return to the Picnic Place.   (P.K. 9/97).

The main street of **Elmley Castle**, *(Walk14)*.

67

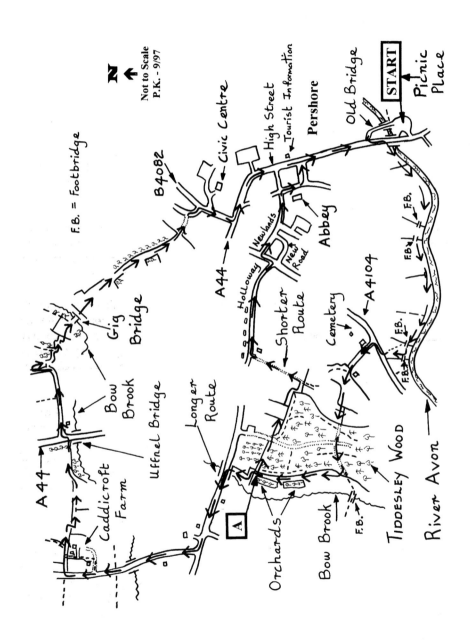

WALK 15   The RIVER AVON, TIDDESLEY WOOD,   4.5 or 7.5 Miles
GIG BRIDGE and PERSHORE

Start: Pershore Bridges Picnic Place, Pershore. (GR. 953451).

Parking: The Picnic Place, (free), or in Pershore, (long stay, chargeable).

Refreshments: Numerous places in Pershore, none on the route.

O.S. Maps: Explorer 14 (Malvern Hills) and Landranger 150 (Worcester).

Summary: A gentle walk along the River Avon and through the Nature
Reserve of Tiddesley Wood. The Longer Route, which involves stretches of road
walking, follows the old route from Drakes Broughton to Pershore via Gig Bridge.
Number of stiles; Shorter Route:- 6, Longer Route:- 10.

General Notes: The historic town of Pershore, with its Norman Abbey, parks,
market and historical buildings, has much to offer the visitor. Whilst the walk goes
through the town centre details have not been included in the text as full information
can be obtained from the Tourist Information Office in the High Street.

Route Notes: From the Picnic Place cross over the old 14th century, (much
repaired), bridge with its mixture of building materials, (note the contrast with the
1926 bridge), and reach the A44. CAREFULLY cross the road, turn left then, just
before the new bridge, take the footpath on the right, (kissing gate), signposted to
Tiddesley Wood. (There are two spellings for the wood, the one in this book is that
used by the owners, the Worcestershire Wildlife Trust).

The first part of the route now follows the River Avon, the footpath going through
another kissing gate and over three footbridges. At various stages along the path the
tower of Pershore Abbey is visible to the right, Bredon Hill, **Walk 14**, is over to the
left, and ahead/right is Tiddesley Wood. (The church spire visible to the right of
Tiddesley Wood is at Pershore Cemetery). After the second footbridge the path
passes through old hedgelines to reach the third footbridge. Cross this, proceed to
the next footbridge but do not cross. Here turn right and follow the left hedge to the
A4104. (This is the correct Right of Way, the path diagonally over the field is not).

Now turn right, go 150 yards and turn left, **carefully** crossing the road, to go up a
tarmac lane, a bridlepath. At the end of the lane, by a thatched cottage, go through
a bridlegate and continue ahead, over the open field. After about 150 yards join a
fence on the right and follow this to the far right corner. Use a stile or gate, then
another after 10 yards, and follow the left hedge to a bridlegate into Tiddesley Wood.

Tiddesley Wood, (spelt Tyddesley on some maps), covers 185 acres, is owned by the Worcestershire Wildlife Trust, and has over 300 types of flowering plants and a large population of birds. There are many permissive paths through the wood, with only a few shown on the map as the route is on Rights of Way. However, the public may normally use all the other paths except for Christmas Day.

For this walk enter the wood and continue ahead on the most prominent path, a bridlepath. Ignore other paths to left and right, cross a forest road and continue on the meandering bridlepath. As an open field is visible through the trees, ahead/right, watch for a narrow path going part right to leave the wood. Enter the field, (broken fence, no stile, in Sept. 1997), and turn right. Follow the edge of the field, trees right and Bow Brook down on the left, (the same Bow Brook as **Walk 12**). Pass orchards on the left and continue to a stile, this is **Point A** on the map and a choice of route.

Shorter Route from Point A: **Do not** cross the stile but turn right and follow the path just inside the wood, an orchard across the ditch to the left. Cross a forest track, (an entry point into Tiddesley Wood), go part left and cross a stile to a field. Now follow the right edge of the field, trees to the right, crossing two more stiles.

At an open field ahead turn right, trees still on the right. At a fence turn left, away from the wood, heading towards Pershore Abbey. Follow the fence for 150 yards to a path junction, here turn left and follow the wide, grassy, track past a barn, to reach a road and turn right. Follow the road to the A4104, turn left for 75 yards, then turn right into Newlands, (which has two pubs!). Follow the road to reach Pershore Abbey Park, then via Broad Street to the A44 and back to the Picnic Place.

Longer Route from Point A: Cross the stile ahead, turn left and cross another stile. Follow the enclosed path for 50 yards, turn right, and continue along a wide grassed area to reach the road. Now turn left and follow the road for some 500 yards, using the grass verges where possible because of the bends in the road.

Turn right into Chevington Lane, (signposted to Drakes Broughton), and follow it for almost one mile to a footpath on the right, about 400 yards past the drive to Caddicroft Farm. Turn right at a very wide metal gate and follow the right ditch and hedge. Go through a hedge gap and continue ahead, passing Caddicroft Farm on the right. (The route via the farm involved 4 stiles so this easier path has been chosen).

Now follow the right fence to a gap some 100 yards past the farm buildings. Go through, turn left, (fence now on the left), and keep the same direction, passing into the next field and still following the left fence. Pass a gap on the left and eventually cross into another field, with a fence and trees now on the right, and follow the fence to the far right corner of the field, (traffic visible ahead on the A44).

In the corner, hidden in the trees some 5 yards from the right fence, are steps up to the A44, (seek and ye shall find). Go up the steps, CAREFULLY cross the A44 and turn left. (To the right is the Ufnell Bridge over Bow Brook, reconstructed in 1934). Go along the A44 for 150 yards and turn right along a tarmac lane, following it to a point some 300 yards after it turns left. Go through an old iron gate on the right, turn right, and follow right hedge. (Yes, this is going back the way you came, but it is the correct Right of Way). After 150 yards go through a gap in the hedge, turn left, pass between open sheds and a fishing pond, and follow the left hedge.

At a 'T' junction turn right and continue following the left hedge as it zigzags around the side of the field. At the second corner cross a stile ahead and go part right down to Gig Bridge over the Bow Brook. Cross a stile, continue ahead to another stile, then cross an open field on a well-defined path. Soon this path becomes a wide track and then follows a tree-hedge on the left, passing through two enclosed sections to reach an estate road. Here turn right to join the B4082 and there turn right to reach the junction with the A44. At the traffic lights turn left, pass through the centre of Pershore and back to the Picnic Place. (P.K. 9/97).

Gig Bridge, *on the Longer Route of **Walk 15**.*

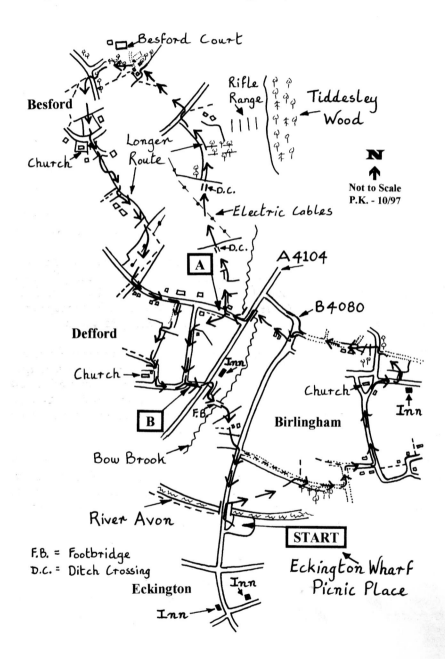

Besford Court

Rifle Range

Tiddesley Wood

Besford

Church

Longer Route

N

Not to Scale
P.K. - 10/97

D.C.

Electric Cables

D.C.

A4104

A

B4080

Defford

Church

Inn

Church

Inn

B

F.B.

Birlingham

Bow Brook

River Avon

START

F.B. = Footbridge
D.C. = Ditch Crossing

Eckington

Inn

Eckington Wharf
Picnic Place

Inn

WALK 16   **BIRLINGHAM, DEFFORD and BESFORD**   **3 or 6 Miles**
              from ECKINGTON WHARF

Start: Eckington Wharf Picnic Place, by Eckington. (GR. 923423).

Parking: At the Eckington Wharf Picnic Place, (free).

Refreshments: Two inns at Eckington. The route also passes within 100 yards
                   of inns at Birlingham and Defford.

O.S. Maps: Explorer 14 (Malvern Hills) and Landranger 150 (Worcester).

Summary: A walk to the villages of Birlingham and Defford, with an
extension to Besford. Number of stiles; Shorter Route:- 10, Longer Route:- 23.

General Notes: This walk links with **Walks 12** and **15** in that they all cross the
Bow Brook, which eventually joins the River Avon to the west of Eckington Bridge.

Route Notes: From the Picnic Place cross the Eckington Bridge over the River
Avon and immediately turn right. Cross a metal stile into the field and go part left,
crossing a large open field, towards the far left corner. (A good aiming point is the
house roof just visible to the left of the taller trees). Cross a stile in the hedge some
50 yards before the taller trees and turn right, joining a wide grassy track.

Follow the track, ignoring other paths off it, to reach a 'T' junction and turn left.
Now follow this wide, and partly stony, track to another 'T' junction and turn right.
Keep on this track, which becomes a tarmac lane, to pass houses and reach a road
'T' junction. Turn left along the road to reach the war memorial and take the right
fork, passing the Parish Church of St. James, on the left. (The church, mainly rebuilt
in the 19th century, is much larger than the first view indicates).

Go just past the church to the telephone box, (still red in October 1997), and turn
right along a lane. Go along the lane for 100 yards then turn left onto a grassy
enclosed path. (The Swan Inn is 100 yards further along the lane). Cross a stile to
a field then go part left, over the open field, to a hedge gap in the far left corner. At
the road turn left, then almost immediately turn right at a road 'T' junction. After
only 30 yards turn left, go up some steps, and cross a fence.

Now go straight ahead, through a small plantation, to a stile. Cross and follow the
metal fence on the left, go through a metal kissing gate, then take the gravel track to
the left of the cattle grid. Follow the track past houses, continue on a part grassy
track and at the B4080 turn left. After 100 yards turn right, over a stile, into a field.

73

Cross the field keeping right of the greenhouses and, after passing the last one, go slightly right, aiming for farm buildings in the middle distance. As a brick bridge comes into view, (on the A4104), keep crossing an open field towards the right end of the bridge. Before reaching the bridge the path sweeps right to join the A4104.

Cross the road and turn left, going over the Bow Brook, (also crossed on **Walks 12 and 15**), and turn right at the road junction, Bluebell Lane. Go up the lane for about 150 yards to just past the farm buildings and a house, this is **Point A** on the map. Please make your choice of route, Shorter Route below, Longer Route on Page 75.

Shorter Route from Point A:

From a point just past the farm building, (right), turn left and go up the bank into a field. Now go part right and across the open field, crops permitting, (**NB, do not** follow the track alongside the hedge on the right), to a stile in the top left corner, (please see the map). (If in doubt aim for the house roofs visible across the field). At the road, (now in Defford), turn left, follow it for 400 yards, then turn left again into Crown Lane. This is **Point B** on the map, the joining point with the Longer route, now see Page 77 and **"Return from Point B"**.

Besford Court, *from the Longer Route of **Walk 16.***

74

The Timber Framed **Besford Church**, *on the Longer Route of* **Walk 16.**

Longer Route from Point A:

From **Point A** turn right, off the road, just past the house, go up a concrete drive and then follow a stony track. Go across an open section of field and then follow a hedge on the left. As the hedge ends go across the open field, on a wide grassy track, to a ditch crossing, (DC), and a stile.

Once over go slightly right, across a large open field, to reach a rather springy DC and a stile in the far hedge. (As a guide pass just to the right of the middle one of the 5 electricity poles going across the field). Now follow the left hedge which curves left to reach a road. (Over to the right is Tiddesley Wood, **Walk 15**, also to the right is a rifle range, so gunfire might be heard on some occasions).

At the road turn right and, after 100 yards, turn left over another stile. Cross another open field aiming for the taller trees on the opposite side. Continue straight ahead, keeping about 50 yards to the right of a bungalow, to cross a stile in a fence. The stile may well be hidden behind undergrowth, (nettles). Enter the grounds of the Besford Court Estate and continue ahead, through an 'overgrown' area, (nettle bashing time again!), aiming for a stone arch.

Go past the left side of the arch, cross over a drive, then continue ahead keeping to the left of a group of trees. (The mansion of Besford Court is visible to the right, beyond the trees). Now keep to the right edge of the field, following the tree line and then a metal fence, on the right, towards the far right corner of the field. Cross a stile, hidden behind some trees, about 20 yards to the left of the corner.

Turn right, along the road, for only 10 yards and cross a stile on the left. Now turn part left and cross the open field, aiming to the right side of the large group of farm buildings. From here, over to the right, the full length of the Malvern Hills are visible. Go over a stile by a water trough and across the field to the far right corner.

Cross the stile to the road and then take the stony track to the left of the telephone box. Over to the right is the Besford Parish Church of St. Peter, with its unusual timber framed nave, dating from the 14th century. Along the road, to the right of the church, there is also the unusual 'crinkle-crankle' wall of Church Farm House.

To continue with the walk, follow the enclosed, stony, track to the left of the telephone box and, on nearing a house, turn right into a field. Now turn left and follow the left fence. After about 100 yards go through a difficult gate on the left, turn right and continue as before with a hedge now on the right. Follow the hedge for some 75 yards and cross a stile on the right. Now turn left, go through an overgrown area, (an ideal place to, yet again, test your nettle bashing skills!), and cross another stile, farm buildings to the right.

Follow the left fence/hedge and continue through a farm machinery 'graveyard' to the far left corner, then cross a stile. After 25 yards cross another stile and turn part right. Pass under some electricity cables to a stile in the far hedge, some 50 yards to the left of the last electricity pole. Turn left at the lane and follow it for some 700 yards. (A possible route directly across the fields was not used as the chosen route offers better views and is much easier to use).

Follow the road to a track on the right, signposted to St. James' Church, (opposite Chattan Lodge). Go along the track to a 'T' junction, (Bredon Hill to the left, Malvern Hills to the right), and turn right. After 30 yards enter another field by a gate or stile and turn left. Follow the left hedge to the far left corner, turn left, then follow the track as it turns right and becomes a tarmac lane, (now back in Defford).

Follow the tarmac lane to pass Defford Parish Church, (St James), on the right. (The church is of Norman origin with a 15th century, half-timbered, tower). Continue to a road 'T' junction and turn left. Now follow the road for 200 yards to Crown Lane and turn right, this is **Point B** on the map. To finish the walk see the next page and the heading, **"Return from Point B"**.

76

Return from Point B:

Go down Crown Lane to the A4104 and cross, going partly left, to a stile by a gate. (The Defford Arms is 100 yards to the left). Follow the right field edge, Bredon Hill, **(Walk 14)**, ahead. Near the bottom right corner go right and follow an enclosed path. Keep alongside the metal fence on the left as it turns left then, as it goes left again, proceed ahead to a footbridge over the Bow Brook.

Once across go part left, over a field, to a stile near a gate. Continue ahead over another open field, going under electric cables and keep to the right of a barn. Cross a farm track, keeping the same direction, and follow a narrow, enclosed, path to cross a stile. Go 100 yards down the field to a stile in the left hedge, by a large metal gate, cross this to reach a road, the B4080.

Here turn right and follow the road back to the Eckington Wharf Picnic Place. (For anyone interested, by using the path on the opposite side of the road from the stile, ramblers can repeat the walk, should they so wish it!). (P.K. 10/97).

Eckington Bridge, *from the* **Eckington Wharf Picnic Place**, *(Walk 16)*.

77

Map for Walk 17   Upton upon Severn and the Severn Way

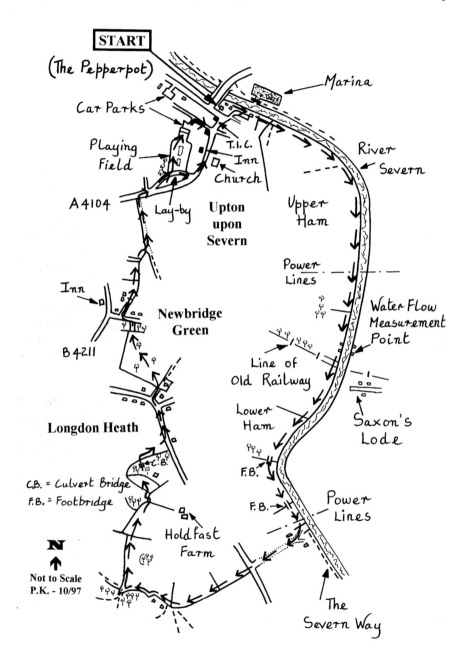

START

(The Pepperpot)

Car Parks

Playing Field

A4104

Marina

T.I.C.
Inn
Church

Lay-by

Upton upon Severn

River Severn

Upper Ham

Power Lines

Inn

B4211

Newbridge Green

Longdon Heath

C.B. = Culvert Bridge
F.B. = Footbridge

N
↑
Not to Scale
P.K. - 10/97

Water Flow Measurement Point

Line of Old Railway

Lower Ham

Saxon's Lode

C.B.

F.B.

Hold fast Farm

F.B.

Power Lines

The Severn Way

WALK 17   UPTON UPON SEVERN and the SEVERN WAY   6 Miles

Start: The 'Pepperpot' at Upton upon Severn, located by the bridge
over the River Severn, (GR. 852407).

Parking: Car Parks in Upton upon Severn, (charge).

Refreshments: Numerous places in Upton upon Severn. On route the 'Drum
and Monkey' is near the end of the walk at Newbridge Green.

O.S. Maps: Explorer 14 (Malvern Hills) and Landranger 150 (Worcester).

Summary: A gentle walk down the River Severn following a small part of the
Severn Way, (see notes on Page 7). The return to Upton upon Severn is mainly on
field paths with a small amount of road walking. Number of stiles:-24.

General Notes: Upton upon Severn, with its waterfront, boats and old buildings
has much to offer, so a visit to the Tourist Information Centre in the High Street is
recommended. The walk, along a small part of the **Severn Way**, passes by two old
ferry points and then returns via Longdon Heath and Newbridge Green.

Route Notes: From the 'Pepperpot', the 13th century Bell Tower of the old
Parish Church of St. Peter and St. Paul, go down to the riverside and walk downstream. (To complete the walk it is advisable, at this early stage, to ignore the many
hostelries!). The first section of the route, until the turn-off away from the river, is
on the **Severn Way**. (Watch for the **Severn Trow** symbol).

Continue past the Swan Hotel, (good view to the Marina on the opposite bank), go
through a bridlegate and follow the riverside path downstream. The large flat area
to the right is known as Upper Ham and, (surprise, surprise!), further down the river
it is Lower Ham. These 'Hams' are areas of flat land, usually partly enclosed by a
river bend, that were once part of the flood plain of the river. The church spire
visible to the right is the 'new' Upton upon Severn Parish Church of St. Peter and
St. Paul, built in the late 19th century to replace the 'old' church, (the 'Pepperpot').

Follow the riverside path downstream, pass under electric cables and then cross a
stile in a fence. After another 300 yards cross two stiles close together, this location
is a water flow measurement point and is also the site of an old railway crossing.
South of this point, between here and the next stile, is the site of an old ferry
crossing. The route was from Saxon's Lode on the east bank of the river, then over
the Lower Ham to Longdon Heath. ('Lode' derives from 'Old English' and means
'way' or 'passage'. 'Saxon' is thought to be the name of a previous ferryman).

79

Continue downstream, cross a stile and a footbridge, and follow the river as it bends to the left. Head towards the houses visible ahead, cross another footbridge and then a stile beneath electric cables. Now turn right, leaving the **Severn Way**, and follow the stony track, past a house, to reach a lane. This track was the route to a medieval river crossing, known latterly as the Uckinghall Ferry.

Cross the lane, go through a gate and follow the left fence. (This route was the continuation of the track from the ferry, and shown as a 'road' on old maps). Cross a stile, going gently uphill along the fence, to the far left corner. Ignore a stile on the left and go over the stile ahead. Pass another stile on the left and follow the left field edge, past houses and trees, to a path junction in the next far left corner.

Now **turn right**, still in the same field, and soon go downhill, the spire of Upton Parish Church visible ahead. (The part timbered building ahead/right is Holdfast Farm). At the bottom left corner of the field cross a stile by a metal gate and go directly over the open field to another stile, also by a metal gate. Once over turn left through a gate, then go immediately right and cross two stiles to enter a field.

Here turn part left and cross the field to a small bridlegate near the far right corner. Go through some trees and over an old culvert bridge. Cross a stile to a field, go part right, and follow a track, (diverging slightly from the trees to the right), to reach a lane. Turn left and follow the lane to the point where it bends left, (Longdon Heath).

The **River Severn** *at* **Upton upon Severn**, *(Walk 17).*

Just past the bend in the road turn right onto a stony track, (The Close), and follow it for 50 yards. Before entering the Village Hall compound go through a gate on the left and then diagonally across the field to the far left corner. Cross a stile, go along an enclosed path, then turn left along a lane, (now in Newbridge Green). Follow this lane for about 150 yards and turn right onto another lane. (For those seeking sustenance the 'Drum and Monkey' is on the B4211; please see the map).

Having turned right into the narrow lane follow it to reach farm buildings, (on the left), and then continue along the right edge of the field. Go through a metal gate and continue ahead, (ditch to the right), and then cross two stiles close together. Follow the right tree line for 50 yards, cross a stile on the right, to join a track and turn left. Keep on the enclosed track to the A4104, carefully cross and turn right.

After some 50 yards take the gentle left fork onto a lay-by, (the old A4104). Part way along the lay-by, at a large metal gate and a kissing gate, there is a choice of route to finish the walk. Either continue ahead, rejoining the A4104 and following it into Upton upon Severn, passing The Upton Muggery Pub, (a The Little Pub Co. pub). Alternatively, turn left at the kissing gate and follow the left edge of a playing field, (this is a Right of Way). At the far end of the playing field go through a children's play area and from there back to the town centre.   (P.K. 10/97).

The **Marina** *at* **Upton upon Severn**, *seen from the* **Severn Way**. *(Walk 17)*.

81

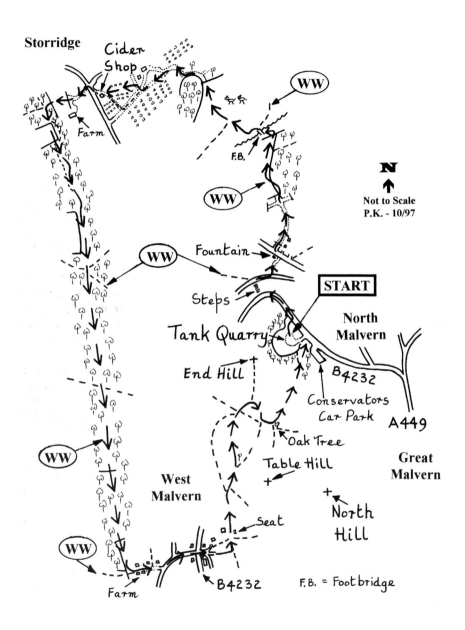

Storridge

Cider Shop

WW

Farm

F.B.

WW

N

↑

Not to Scale
P.K. - 10/97

WW   Fountain

Steps

WW

Tank Quarry

End Hill

WW

West Malvern

Seat

WW

Farm   B4232

START

North Malvern

B4232

Conservators
Car Park   A449

Oak Tree

Table Hill   Great Malvern

+
North
Hill

F.B. = Footbridge

WALK 18   NORTH and WEST MALVERN via STORRIDGE   4.5 Miles

Start: Tank Quarry Picnic Place, signposted off the B4232, in North
                    Malvern, (GR. 768470).

Parking: At Tank Quarry, (as above, free, note opening times), or at the
                    nearby Malvern Hills Conservators car park, (chargeable).

Refreshments: Numerous places in Malvern. The route also goes past the farm
                    shop of Knights Cider Co., (open Friday to Sunday), where the
                    local cider can be purchased to accompany your own picnic.

O.S. Maps: Explorer 14 (Malvern Hills) and Landranger 150 (Worcester).

Summary: An undulating walk north of the Malvern Hills to Storridge, using
parts of the **Worcestershire Way**, **(WW)**, and crossing the border between
Worcestershire and Herefordshire. The paths used are within the Malvern Hills Area
of Outstanding Natural Beauty. However, the route deliberately avoids the main
spine of the hills where there are serious erosion problems. Number of stiles:- 8.

General Notes: Tank Quarry was part of a group of quarries, known as Pyx
Quarries, and ceased operation in 1970. It takes its name from a water tank, built in
1835, to supply water to residents in the area. The site has been landscaped by the
County Council as a Picnic Place, an access point to the Malvern Hills and a link to
the **WW**, (see Page 7). It has an interesting display of geological information.

Route Notes: From the main car parking area take the path going north, signposted 'WW and picnic area', join the B4232 and turn left. Follow it, views right
over the Worcestershire Plain, to where the road bends left. Here take a footpath on
the right that goes down a steep flight of steps to another road. Ignore the stile
opposite and turn right, now joining the **WW**, (**Pear** symbol), going north.

Follow the road for some 100 yards then turn left, via a stile, onto an enclosed footpath, going downhill to reach another road. Now turn left, (notice the fountain
presented by William, Earl Beauchamp, to the people of Cowleigh in 1905). Follow
the road for about 75 yards and turn right, via an iron gate, to follow a stony track.
Keep on this track, buildings to the right, to go through a bridlegate and then sweep
left to reach a path junction. (Still following the **WW** and the **Pear** symbol).

At a path junction keep directly ahead into the trees then, after 30 yards, take a
narrow path on the right that keeps just inside the tree line. Cross a stile and soon
join a field, following the right edge to reach the bottom right corner.

83

Now please have your passports ready! Cross the stile ahead, turn left and then proceed to, and cross, a footbridge over a small stream. The stream is the boundary between Worcestershire and Herefordshire.

Once over the bridge turn left, (leaving the **WW**), follow the stream for 50 yards, then turn right and walk up the hill towards the trees at the top. (There is no real aiming point, my wife did suggest two cows on the hill; these were not considered to be a permanent enough fixture to use as a guide!). Soon join an easily followed grassy track that goes up the hill, sweeping gently right, to cross a stile by a gate.

Now follow the initially enclosed track, through trees, as it sweeps left, leaves the trees and sweeps right. Keep on this wide, twisting track, pass through the end of an orchard, (the right fork goes to the farmhouse), and at a concrete drive turn left.

Go 30 yards along the drive and turn right onto another concrete drive. After approx. 40 yards go part left, leaving the drive to cross the grass and go through a small section of orchard. Soon join a track that leads to the Knights Cider Co. Farm Shop, where the local cider can be bought. (The route described above is the Right of Way, there is also a permissive route along tracks, this is shown on the map).

The shop, normally open Friday to Sunday, allows prospective purchasers to sample the cider before buying. There are also fruit wines available for sale. This is an ideal place for a picnic with 'on tap' liquid refreshment.

The Farm Shop of **Knights Cider Company**, *(**Walk 18**)*.

After 'shampling' (hic!) the 'shyder' (hic!) continue to the road, VERY CAREFULLY cross, and take the footpath, (wide track), going gently uphill towards Whitman's Hill Farm. At the top of the drive cross a stile to a field, go slightly right, and up the field to a wide makeshift stile to enter the wood.

Proceed ahead into the wood for 50 yards then, at a path cross-roads, turn left. After 100 yards cross a stile into a field and follow the left fence. (This path is the Right of Way, the path that stays in the wood is not. Also, ramblers should not look right to avoid being enticed by the seductive beauty of Herefordshire). Cross a stile back onto the wood and keep on the more prominent path going ahead/left, continuing through coppiced woodland. (If muddy there is a narrower path on the right).

The route now goes through woodland, for just over one mile, going in a southerly direction. At one point the path follows a fence, on the right, with views across Herefordshire, crosses over a path 'cross-roads' and then rejoins the **Worcestershire Way**. (At this junction keep directly ahead and **do not** use the path going off to the left). Stay on the **WW**, passing over another path junction and through two gates to reach a field, (a farm implement 'graveyard'), with West Malvern and North Hill ahead/left. Go to the bottom right corner of the field and turn **left**, leaving the **WW**.

Follow the wide, muddy, track through a farmyard, (now back in Worcestershire). At the road turn left and follow it, (Croft Bank), as it sweeps right and gently uphill to reach the B4232. Cross this and go uphill on a tarmac lane/path to a 'T' junction and turn left, now on the lower slopes of Table Hill. (There is a useful seat on this track to rest and contemplate the completion of the walk).

As there is a plethora of paths over the Malvern Hills, the route described from here to Tank Quarry is the shortest one using Rights of Way. Ramblers with the appropriate map should feel free to use whichever route they wish.

For this walk follow the wide track going north, pass a house on the left, and at a fork keep right, going gently uphill. Ignore a track going sharp right and up the hill then, at the next fork keep left, on a level path, heading in the direction of End Hill.

At a junction of numerous paths initially head towards End Hill and then sweep around to the right without starting to go uphill. Very soon turn left to go down a steep slope to reach a path 'cross-roads' by an isolated oak tree. Here turn left and follow the valley track, with a view ahead over the Worcestershire Plain. The track continues downhill and on reaching the old quarry workings becomes stony. Ignore a narrow track going off to the left, continue going downhill, eventually descending a series of steps to reach the B4232 by the entrance to Tank Quarry. (P.K. 10/97).

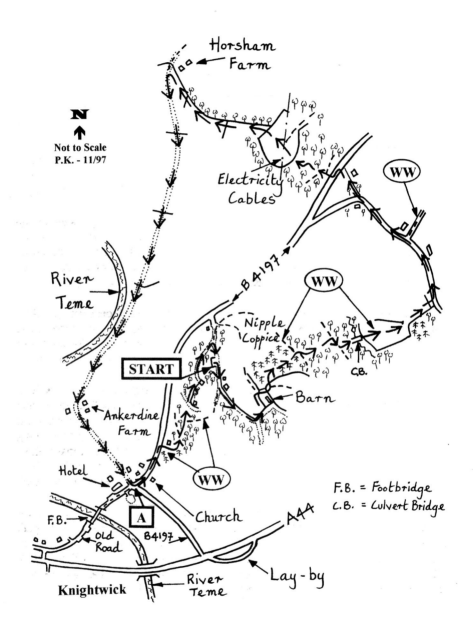

Horsham Farm

N

Not to Scale
P.K. - 11/97

WW

Electricity
Cables

River
Teme

B 4197

WW

Nipple
Coppice

START

C.B.

Barn

Ankerdine
Farm

WW

Hotel

F.B. = Footbridge
C.B. = Culvert Bridge

F.B.

A

Church

A44

Old
Road

B4197

Lay-by

Knightwick

River
Teme

ANKERDINE HILL and KNIGHTWICK   3.5 Miles

Start: The Ankerdine Common Picnic Place, off the B4197, just north of Knightwick. (GR. 737567). See also **General Notes**, below.

Parking: At the Picnic Place but see also **General Notes**, below.

Refreshments: The Talbot Hotel at Knightwick.

O.S. Maps: Pathfinder 995 (Bromyard) and Landranger 150 (Worcester).

Summary: An undulating walk linking Ankerdine Hill, Horsham and Knightwick that can seem longer than only 3.5 miles. It does, however, offer views over Worcestershire, and the Teme Valley towards Herefordshire, as well as using a small part of the **Worcestershire Way, (WW)**. Number of stiles:- 9 (maximum).

General Notes: Ankerdine Common Picnic Place, (limited parking), is by the top of Ankerdine Hill, so routes from it are 'down', and routes back are 'up'. If not wishing to finish the walk going uphill, it can be started from **Point A**, by The Talbot Hotel, **(car park for patrons only)**. Parking possible at a lay-by on the A44 or the old road by the footbridge over the River Teme, (see the map **and** Page 89).

Route Notes: From the parking area take the wide track, going gently uphill. After 100 yards, immediately past a dwelling, turn left down the side of the house, (leaving the **WW**). Follow the partly sunken track, fence on the left, downhill with views left over Worcestershire. At a path junction turn left, heading towards a barn.

Just prior to the barn cross a stile on the left. Follow the right fence, barn on right, for 40 yards and go through a gate on the right. Go through a small enclosure and another gate, turn left, then through gate into a wood, (now Nipple Coppice but last century known as Dean's Woods). (The 'Definitive Map' shows the path entering the wood some 100 yards down the field, however, there is no trace of that path so this point of entry has been used). Follow the track as it meanders through conifers to reach a 'T' junction, broad leafed trees ahead, there turn right, rejoining the **WW**.

Follow the **WW**, (keep on the prominent track and watch for the **Pear** symbol), for about 250 yards to reach another 'T' junction and turn right. (**NB**, do not take a path going to the right at a slight 'dog-leg' in the main path). Now follow this, often muddy, track for about 150 yards and take a narrower path going left, (still the **WW**). Go down to a culvert bridge over a stream, cross a stile into a field, then go part right and up the field to head towards the left end of a pine wood.

Now follow the right fence, go through two gates to a lane and turn left, following the lane for some 300 yards to a road junction. Here keep left, leaving the **WW**, and continue up the lane for about 350 yards. Opposite a house on the left take an enclosed track going off to the right and follow it, up some steepish sections, to the B4197. Turn left, following the road for only 50 yards and turn right into the wood.

Once into the wood follow the most prominent path, meandering downhill through the trees to a stile to a field. (Look for the yellow marks on the trees to keep on the right path). Cross the stile, (view ahead over the Teme Valley to Herefordshire), go slightly right, and pass an electricity pole to a stile, by a gate, near the far left corner.

Now follow a wide track, a hedge, (of trees), on the right, as it meanders downhill through two more gates, (or stiles), to reach Horsham Farm. Here turn left and follow a long stony track, going away from the farm. Proceed via three gates, (purists will use the stiles instead), and eventually reach the River Teme.

Continue on the track, River Teme to the right, (at this point the river is the boundary between Worcestershire and Herefordshire), and then leave the river to pass through Ankerdine Farm. Now join a concrete drive that leads to the B4197 and the Talbot Hotel, Knightwick. This is **Point A** on the map, a starting point for those people parking off the A44. (The old road bridge over the River Teme, now replaced by a footbridge, was referred to, on old maps, as Knightsford Bridge).

The Talbot Hotel, Knightwick, *and* **Ankerdine Hill,** *(Walk 19).*

88

To Ankerdine Hill from Point A: From The Talbot Hotel proceed **uphill** on the B4197, joining the **WW**. Pass the small Parish Church of St. Mary's on the right, (built in the mid 19th century), and continue up the hill for a further 300 yards. (Be careful, fast traffic). Now watch for, and take, a footpath going off to the right, (by a cottage), and into the trees, (still the **WW**).

The path now enters Ankerdine Common, which has a set of by-laws issued by the County Council in 1909 and confirmed by the Secretary of State in 1910. It is expected that these will be updated sometime in the near future. (Ramblers with the time and inclination can study the notice situated at the entrance to the wood). Go into the trees for 50 yards then turn sharp left, continuing uphill. At a fork in the track keep to the right hand path which continues uphill.

At the next path junction keep straight ahead, **leaving** the **WW** which goes off to the right. Cross a drive and continue past the house, (on the right), re-entering the trees. On reaching another stony drive keep ahead, going away from a house. After about 100 yards turn sharp right to follow the 'red-brick road' back to the Ankerdine Common Picnic Place. (P.K. 11/97).

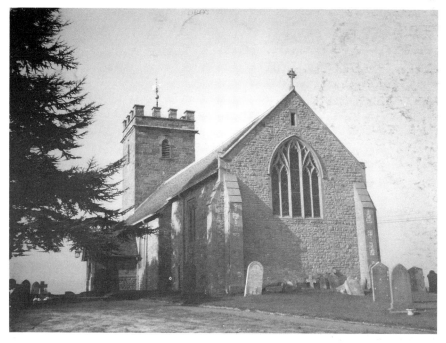

Bayton Parish Church, *(Walk 20).*

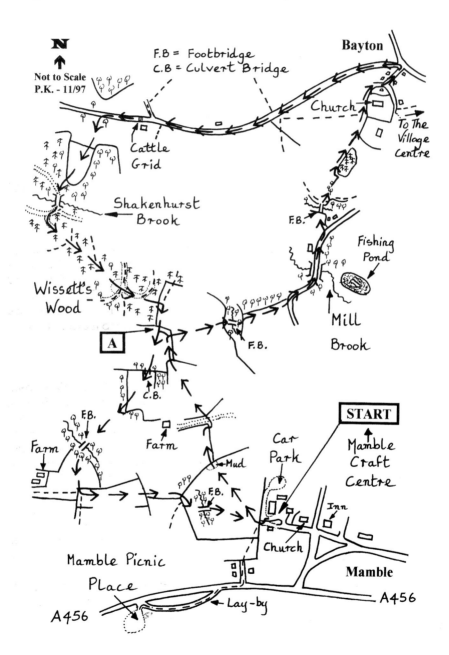

WALK 20   MAMBLE, BAYTON and WISSETT'S WOOD   1.5 or 4 Miles

Start: Mamble Craft Centre, at Mamble, off the A456. (GR. 688717).

Parking: At the Mamble Craft Centre, but please use the rear car park, or at the Picnic Place at the lay-by on the A456. (See the map).

Refreshments: At the Craft Centre or the 'Sun and Slipper', none on the route.

O.S. Maps: Pathfinder map 952 (Wyre Forest and Cleobury Mortimer) and Landranger map 138 (Kidderminster).

Summary: A gentle walk through countryside near the Shropshire border, the Longer Route going to Bayton and Wissett's Wood. The route uses cross-field and woodland paths, and minor roads. There are some very muddy parts so please wear appropriate footwear. Number of stiles; Shorter Route:- 8, Longer Route:- 15.

General Notes: The Mamble Craft Centre, (not normally open on Mondays except Bank Holidays, see also advert. on Page 94), is a renovated barn, and the owners have agreed to allow ramblers doing this walk to park there. (Please use the rear car park). An alternative car park is the County Council's Mamble Picnic Place at the lay-by on the A456, please see the map. Mamble Parish Church, (St. John the Baptist), dating from the early 13th century, is by the entrance to the Craft Centre.

Route Notes:

Mamble Picnic Place to the Craft Centre: From the Picnic Place return to the lay-by, follow it eastwards to the A456 and continue eastwards for 50 yards, crossing the road where appropriate. Turn left along a track between houses, go over a stile and cross the field to a gate. Now go part right to a stile in the right fence. To visit the Craft Centre cross the stile and soon use another stile, on the left, to the Craft Centre grounds. If going direct to the church continue along the enclosed path, past a cottage, to a lane by the Craft Centre entrance, the church is then ahead/left.

Route Notes from the Craft Centre: From a position facing the front of the Craft Centre go to the left of the building and cross a 'permissive' stile in the left fence and turn right. Cross a stile into a field and go part right, then diagonally over the field, to a gate. (**NB**, the area by this gate can be very muddy).

Once through the gate, (and the mud!), follow the right hedge to a gate at the far right corner. Go through, cross a stony track, then through another gate into a field. Now go part left to go through yet another gate near the far left corner.

Follow the right hedge to a stile some 30 yards before reaching the far right corner, the **Longer Route crosses** this stile. (For the Shorter Route **do not** cross this stile but turn part left, to go to a stile some 50 yards left of the right hand corner, this is **Point A** on the map. **Do not** cross this second stile but turn around and see the notes on Page 93, **"Route Notes from Point A"**). For the Longer Route see below.

Longer Route, (from near Point A):   Having crossed the stile in the right fence go slightly left, across a large open field, (usually with crops). If the path is not marked, (hard luck if you are the first to walk the route after ploughing!), aim for the right end of the tree line, as visible from this position, on the far side of the field. Once over the field look for a feint path going into the trees, about 30 yards to the left of a large tree in the hedge. Follow the path down to a footbridge and cross.

Now go up a bank, cross a stile, then follow the left edge of the field, (Mamble church spire visible to the right), go over a stile to the road and turn left. Cross the bridge over Mill Brook and keep on the road, which turns left, for about 350 yards past the bridge. Now cross a stile on the left, (about 50 yards before reaching a brick cottage), go part right, (past sheds on the right), to a stile in the tree line.

Cross two stiles, concrete footbridge between, and continue **ahead**, up the hill, past three trees and then over an open field to a small wood. The 'Definitive Map' indicates that the 'Right of Way' goes through the wood. As this is not possible the suggested route is around the left side of the wood to the gate to Bayton Church. (Once up the hill the view on this side is toward the Clee Hills).

St. Bartholomew's has Norman origins with later additions and alterations, there are good views towards Shropshire and the Clee Hills. From the front entrance to the churchyard it is possible to go, via footpath or road, to the centre of Bayton village, (interesting old Drinking Fountain dated 1937). Alas, the village Inn, (The Wheatsheaf), has now closed, so there is no place for liquid refreshment.

To continue the walk, follow the church wall, (on the right), then a hedge, and on reaching a lane turn left. At a road junction turn sharp right into a lane marked "Private Road". The sign is correct, it is a private road but it is also a Right of Way, a bridlepath. This lane is now followed for about one mile, a possible diversion from it was not used as hedges had been removed and the route across open fields was tedious. The road is, however, pleasant for walking, with views to the Clee Hills.

Eventually cross a cattle grid by a cottage, follow lane for a further 400 yards, then turn left just past a large oak tree. Cross a stile in the fence ahead and go down the hill to a stile near the bottom right corner. Now go part left to a forest road, turn left and cross the bridge over Shakenhurst Brook, then at a 'T' junction turn right.

Follow this track for only 20 yards and turn left onto a grassy, (and often muddy), uphill track. Soon it sweeps left, levels out, and meanders through Wissett's Wood, (watch for Bluebells in Spring). Ignore other tracks off it and, at a path junction, (small clearing and log gathering point), continue straight ahead, now on a stony track. As this track sweeps left leave it and continue ahead to a gate in the fence. Go through, or around, the gate into a field and turn right, then follow the field edge to a stile and cross to the next field. This is **Point A** on the map, now see below.

Route Notes from Point A: With your back to the stile go slightly right and over the field towards the timber framed farmhouse. Cross a stile by a gate, and a culvert bridge, then go part right, over the open field, to another stile by a gate. Now go part left, down the field, (aim to the left of the farm buildings across the valley), to a footbridge, (loose handrail in Nov. 1997), hidden in the trees. Once over go part left, through the trees, to a field. At the field edge again go part left, across the field, to a stile at approx. the mid-point of the opposite hedge.

Cross the stile, by a gate, go to the left, and head directly towards the Mamble Craft Centre. Cross a stile by a water trough and follow the right hedge to a gate near the far right end of the field. Once through go part left to reach a footbridge over a brook. Now go directly over the field to the stile to the right of the Craft Centre and then to the Tea Room for some well-earned refreshment.   (P.K. 11/97).

The **Mamble Craft Centre**, *(Walk 20).*

Other **Walking Books** by **Peter Kerr**

□□□□□□□□□□□□□□□□□□□□□□□□□□□□□□□□□□

"Walks Around **Bewdley** and the **Wyre Forest**"

£3-95

A 64 page book of **15** circular and linear walks, ranging from
3 to **7** miles, from **car parks** and **Picnic Places** in, and
around, **Bewdley**. The walks start from **Bewdley, Blackstone,**
the **Wyre Forest Visitor Centre** located at Callow Hill,
Hawkbatch and the **Habberley Valley.**

****

"Walks Around The Severn Valley"

£4-95

An 80 page book of **15** circular walks, from **2** to **8** miles,
along **The Severn Valley** between **Bridgnorth** and
Stourport-on-Severn, linking with most stations on the
Severn Valley Railway. The walks start from river crossings
located at **Bridgnorth, Hampton Loade, Alveley/Highley,**
Upper Arley, Bewdley and **Stourport.**

Available from most **Bookshops** and **Tourist Information**
Centres in the **West Midlands**. Also from **Severn Valley**
Railway stations.

In case of difficulty, copies also available direct from the Author at:-
Dunley Cottage, Dowles Road, Bewdley, Worcs., DY12 2EJ.

(Please add £0-55p for postage and packing)

NOW OPEN

The Famous French
SUPERB

Café René

Le Pub
Avec
Le Grub

On the A449 Kidderminster to Wolverhampton Rd. at Cookley

Vive La Difference!

**01562
850311**